the taste of silence

how i came to be at home with myself

Bieke Vandekerckhove

Translated from the Dutch by
Rudolf V. Van Puymbroeck

Foreword by
Ton Lathouwers

LITURGICAL PRESS
Collegeville, Minnesota

www.litpress.org

Originally published by Uitgeverij Ten Have, Utrecht

Cover design by Jodi Hendrickson. Cover photo: Dreamstime.

The Library of Congress has cataloged the printed edition as follows:

Library of Congress Cataloging-in-Publication Data

Vandekerckhove, Bieke.
[Smaak van stilte. English]
The taste of silence : how I came to be at home with myself / Bieke Vandekerckhove ; translated from the Dutch by Rudolf V. Van Puymbroeck.
pages cm
Includes bibliographical references.
ISBN 978-0-8146-4773-8 — ISBN 978-0-8146-4799-8 (ebook)
1. Spirituality. 2. Spiritual life. I. Title.
BL624.V34513 2015
204'.4—dc23 2015003707

For Gaby, who taught me to live "the great silence,"
and for Bart, my love and companion on the journey.

do not close the windows

soon it will enter

the greatest silence.

J. C. van Schagen

contents

foreword to the Dutch edition ix
Ton Lathouwers

preface xiii

1. to fall 1
2. thinking doesn't do it 5
3. the spark that lives within 9
4. light without form 19
5. new year's wish 26
6. out of boredom 33
7. strangely familiar 39
8. jump into not-knowing 44
9. and still not-knowing 50
10. things as things 55
11. what confuses 61
12. my desert 66
13. ever . . . 68
14. going against gravity 73
15. tsimtsum 77
16. room for the unfamiliar 84
17. up to here and not farther? 89
18. stretched out in the grass 94

19. nobody's breath 99

20. troublesome companions 104

21. live your questions now 106

22. the one seat 111

23. being at home with yourself 117

24. to practice for others 123

25. bull power 128

26. not the winter but the duration 134

27. short story about love 142

glossary 147

bibliography 149

websites 154

translator's note 155

foreword to the Dutch edition

The first image that comes to me, now that I am writing this foreword to Bieke Vandekerckhove's book, is that of the wall. This image has stayed with me ever since I first encountered it in Dostoevsky, some sixty years ago. Ten years later, when I was studying Slavic languages, it showed up again in my favorite Russian-Jewish author, Lev Shestov. In Shestov's work I encountered the phrase that "every authentic search ends in a lonely path, and that all lonely paths inevitably end at a wall." Another ten years later I came across this "wall" again in classic Zen literature, the best-known collection of which is aptly called *Wall without Gates*.

This image of the wall runs like a red thread through *the taste of silence*, even though Bieke does not say so explicitly. Perhaps I can best clarify its meaning by giving two citations. The first is from Dostoevsky's novel *Notes from the Underground*, the second is borrowed from the final chapter of *Wall without Gates*:

> One can understand everything, have insight into everything, every impossibility and every stone wall, and yet not resign oneself to a single one of these impossibilities and stone walls.
>
> Don't be surprised that walls without gates prove to be so difficult and that they trigger intense anger in Zen monks!

In one of the chapters of the book, Bieke expresses in a particularly moving way what is referred to in these quotations. It's the chapter in which she talks frankly about her own experience in hitting the wall, in coming to a dead end that appears impossible to accept, but at the same time, realizing that this "dead end" must never be allowed to have the last word. Bieke uses an impressive quotation from French author Sylvie Germain about the insufficiency and the impotence of current religious language when faced with this "dead end." The biblical figure of Job occupies a central role for her. Job perfectly reflects what is meant about the wall in the two quotations above: anger, rebellion, a holy nonacceptance and nonacquiescence, and, especially, a refusal of every attempt at explanation and justification of what is unacceptable.

And precisely there, in the apparently senseless screaming and raging of Job, may lie an unexpected opening. Precisely here one can fall silent—*To Fall Silent* is also the title of a movie about Bieke—the unconditional option for silence as the only way that remains. For me, Bieke's quotation from Sylvie Germain is one of the most impressive expressions of witness in her book. It translates her own yelling, her own revolt against the wall, and finally her own entering into the silence, the silence of Zen meditation with which she has become familiar now for so many years.

This is the other image of the wall, the wall that can never be conquered with words and violence. This is the other image of the wall that stands at the beginning of the Zen tradition. It is said of the legendary founder of Zen Buddhism, Bodhidharma, that he sat in meditation in front of a wall for a full nine years before finally breaking his silence. This is how he expressed his own waiting and vigil in silence and mindfulness, his own not-knowing and his own, based on nothing, primal confidence that the wall does not constitute the last word, that no wall constitutes the last word.

At one time Bieke told me that it was exactly the confrontation with the wall that taught her to look for what she called the "deepest reality." What I found particularly moving was the fact that she translated the abstract-sounding "deepest reality" in a manner that rendered it concrete and immediate. I'll never forget her reaction to a Russian story I told her about a dying young soldier in the Second World War who, just before he passed away, only had interest in a blue dragonfly that flew above the water close to him. She recognized immediately that the seemingly incomprehensible captivation of this dying boy by something so simple was a profound revelation at the edge of eternity. "Yes, so common and at the same time so uncommon is the deepest reality," she wrote me.

There is also a whole other way in which Bieke appears to be extremely close to the deepest reality. Time and again she forgets her own suffering when she sees the difficulties of others. By a fortuitous set of circumstances in the past few weeks I witnessed this myself. Acting in this way, she expresses, in a manner that serves as an example to me and many others, what is most essential in Mahayana Buddhism, of which the Zen tradition is a part. The deepest reality is not, as is so often supposed, an engagement with our own well-being but, rather, the fact that our own deliverance—whatever that may mean—is unconditionally connected with the deliverance of the "other." This is summarized in a short and powerful manner in the so-called "First vow of the Bodhisattva," which is recited daily in all Zen temples: "No matter how numerous the living beings may be, I commit to liberate them all."

That is not the only way in which Bieke serves as an example to me. I also want to mention her drive, her courage, her radiating joy, and the many activities that she has taken on despite all limitations. Bieke leads a meditation group, writes articles, carries on an extensive correspondence, and now publishes her book.

Her work *the taste of silence* is for me a particularly authentic and deep witnessing of the humanly "impossible" that human beings are capable of. At the same time, the book expresses, in contemporary and lively language, a quest that many people will recognize. It is a quest in which the recurring themes are hope and fear, doubt and—even more so—faith against all evidence, longing, and especially love and compassion. The witness that the author gives to all of this can, I am deeply convinced, be a guide for many on their own inner journey.

The author's familiarity with Buddhism and Judeo-Christianity, the two great religious traditions that encounter each other ever more frequently these days, adds an extra dimension to this guide. Psalms and sutras, prayer and silent meditation, verbal expression and fundamental not-knowing, all make a regular appearance, standing shoulder to shoulder, maintaining thereby their own unique value, and—certainly equally important—they are always approached with an attitude that is as critical as it is open.

Throughout all of this, ultimately what mainly resounds is Bieke's witness to what was referred to in the above quotations about the wall: the primordial confidence that exists despite everything and that appears to be based on nothing, which is also expressed in the language of the psalms, a language particularly dear to the author: "with the help of the Eternal One I can surmount even the highest wall."

Ton Lathouwers

preface

One does not write to be published,
one writes to breathe.

Samuel Beckett

This book has its origin in my life's journey. When I was a nineteen-year-old psychology student, I fell ill. The diagnosis was harsh and inexorable: amyotrophic lateral sclerosis. Cause: unknown. Treatment: nonexistent. Probability of cure: zero. Life expectancy: two to five years. Course: progressive paralysis of the muscles, respiratory difficulties, trouble swallowing, leading to death. There's the sum total of what I had to deal with. How do you survive something like that? What do you do when all that's left is a paltry bit of life? Circumstances led me to an abbey. The quiet of the place moved me. I decided to live the short time I had left with the Benedictine sisters, in accord with the rhythm of the silence. There I became familiar with the spirituality of Benedict and with praying the psalms. It influenced my life for good.

My physical condition kept deteriorating until, after about three years, the doctor gave me a variant of the good news/bad news routine. The good news: as inexplicably as the illness had started, it had gone into remission. The bad news: it could start up again at any time and, of course, I would never get better. Again I had to pick myself up and begin to build a new life with a damaged body. Where to start when you practically can't do anything? My arms are just about completely paralyzed, so I can do nothing on my own. I need continual help with the simplest things: eating, drinking, washing up, putting on a coat, and so on. It has taken a lot of effort, but I have now been living with ALS for twenty years. I am married and have two personal assistants to help me with all daily activities.

During the last ten years I came upon the silence of Zen. I got to know the Maha Karuna Ch'an with Zen teacher Ton Lathouwers. That encounter proved decisive.

The chapters in this book reflect what I have experienced, seen, and tasted in the stillness of life. Benedictine spirituality and Zen Buddhism play a constant role. They have become the two lungs through which I breathe. They are my two major sources of inspiration. The situation in which I found myself forced me into "no-action" and many hours of silence. Nothing was more difficult. But I discovered that there is nothing more dynamic. Everything that happens in that silence is what this book is all about. It brings together a number of pieces written over a course of years. A few were published previously, sometimes under a different form, in various periodicals. The pieces are not arranged chronologically. While each text can be read on its own, together they form a whole, like a puzzle.

It is with much trepidation that I let go of these reflections. I hope they reach people who, just like me, have been touched by the taste of silence.

I thank the Trappists of Saint Sixtus Abbey in Westvleteren and the Benedictine sisters of Saint-Lioba Convent in Egmond-Binnen for their hospitality over the years. I thank the many monks and religious who crossed my path in Zevenkerken, Zundert, Bethanië, and Chevetogne. I want to mention by name Abbot Remi, Br. Godfried, Br. Johannes, Br. Benoît, Br. Andrew, Sr. Karin, and Sr. Zoë. I am grateful to the Maha Karuna Ch'an in Steyl and the Zen sangha in Ghent with Zen teacher Frank De Waele for giving me the opportunity to connect deeply with Zen, notwithstanding severe physical limitations. I thank the many "co-sitters." It gives me pleasure to name Fernanda and Geert, who opened the door to Zen. Also Nicole, Louise, Pat, Karin, Hilde, Geert, Liliane, and Lut who assist me whenever necessary. I want to thank Ton for his humor and depth, and for encouraging this writing adventure; my parents for their trust in the life they gave me; my family and friends for the encounters that make life meaningful. My thanks also to Jenny Dejager for allowing me to use one of her poetic images for the title of this book. Finally, I also want to thank Bart, my husband, my first reader and soundboard, my puzzler without whom this book would never have seen the light of day.

Bieke Vandekerckhove

"Resilience," Els Vermandere
(photo: Benoit Goffart)

to fall

A scared bird
moribund
frozen
perched
on a withered branch.
Frail support
like empty words.

Where leads the doubt?
Who breaks its fall?

Jenny Dejager

Scared to death. Exhausted. Broken. Lost. Angry. Inconsolable. In an infinite, indifferent universe, I feel endlessly alone. Horrible!

And then the burden of your body. So much of a burden that you don't dare go to the doctor. Not yet. When you fear the worst, that's what happens. Stick your head in the sand just a bit longer, 'cause you can't tolerate bad news. Not yet.

In the meantime, you're climbing up the walls. You don't feel good anywhere. Again and again you swallow the lump in your throat . . . until you can't anymore, and the lake behind your eyes seems bottomless.

Everything loses its glow. Nothing makes sense anymore.

The things that used to preoccupy you for days on end, how silly they all appear!

Fear. A searing pain in the soul. Panic. While that one oppressive question keeps hammering in my head: How much time do I have left? How do I manage this without losing my mind?

Even now, eye to eye with the aggression of the incurable illness, from somewhere an odd realization bubbles up against the thought of committing euthanasia: no act is without consequences. You have responsibilities. Even now. Not for what happens. What happens to you, you don't have control over. But how you handle it . . . That, yes! Whether or not you carry on makes a big difference for those around you. And, also, how you carry on. Oosterhuis shows the way: handle your sorrow in such a way that it does not isolate or embitter you. Stay connected. With others. With God. "Yours is the future, come what may." Fine words. Hard to live with. I'll do my best. But I don't know if I can pull it off.

Suddenly, severe doubt. I fall . . . Will there be somebody to catch me on the other side of this life? Then there's the realization that an infinite number of people have fallen before me, throughout the ages. Who catches them? Or the equally infinite number of people who are falling around me, all over the world. Is there really something that saves us?

If there is nothing, then this life is no more than an absurd, deeply tragic accident—the blind consequence of an equally blind evolution in which people, animals, and things are pitilessly sacrificed to the jaws of an insatiable evolutionary principle. Not an attractive proposition!

Unexpectedly, some consolation from a phrase in a Buddhist text. About the deliverance of all living beings. Even the smallest plant or blade of grass . . . There has to be something, whatever it may be. But when you're falling, this gives you nothing to hold on to.

I fall ever lower. I can't figure it out. I know nothing anymore. I am only capable of despair, and a deep cry for help. This is our rawest, most intimate self, I think. To fall. To doubt. To want to believe with all your heart. To be unable to. And to cry out for help . . .

A friend told me that believing precisely consists in this: throwing yourself backward into the abyss and shouting for help. I had to laugh, despite my distress. He is not thin, by any means. I am skin over bones. With his talk of falling and jumping, I suddenly felt transported into the world of Toon Tellegen's animal stories. As if my friend were the elephant, I the ant, and together we were doing an exercise in falling. And perhaps our life is indeed like these stories. Because the animals of Toon Tellegen don't know a thing. At least if by *knowing* you mean: "to have a perfect explanation." They just try this and that. They have high jinks. They err miserably. They are a disorderly bunch. And yet Tellegen ends and begins their story with: "Perhaps they knew everything." The animals of Toon Tellegen, they dare: to jump and to fall, into the abyss, toward the unknown.

To fall. A shout. A longing, too. To come clean with everything. That also. The rest fades away. It no longer matters at all. To come clean . . . . With what you did to others. With what others did to you. I find that in the face of death you want to give and receive forgiveness. Strange.

Death is the great unknown. We approach it *naked*. With empty hands. Alone and defenseless. "Death is the only thing that is just," my physical therapist likes to say. "It's the only thing that is the same for everyone." "It is then that you have to stand on your own two legs," sings Willem Vermandere. That's all well and good. But today it does not console me either.

I am scared to death of the eventual decline. Of the thousand things I need to let go. Of the absolute unknown. Of saying farewell to the face that I cannot and do not want to miss, because I have grown into it so intimately. There is a poem that says: "It's nice to be a house for the only heart you don't want to leave behind." I didn't realize it, but love is a house. Friendship is a path—a wonderful combination of paths, that sometimes diverge considerably, and of intersections. Love, on the other hand, is a house. It has to do with "under one roof." If day after day the two of you share the same house, share your meals, share life, love, and pain . . . you grow into each other. If night after night you sleep side by side, you become closely bonded. I am beginning to understand what it means to become "one flesh." Your life can become entwined with that of another on many levels. You can have such an intense history together that you can't imagine your life separate from the other. If you really love someone, you cannot and you do not want to die, just as you do not want the other to die. Love wants to be a house that spans beyond death. Love hurts terribly.

thinking doesn't do it

Thinking leads no more
to your true origin,
than boiling sand
will give you rice.

Buddha

"Go stand where there is no place to stand" says the *koan* of modern Japanese Zen master Hisamatsu. For me, I had no choice in the matter. I was flung onto that place. Life forced me onto a place where I did not want to stand at all.

I had always been a busy bee. Until I became paralyzed in my arms and all of a sudden became unable to do anything at all. Done with studying. Done with my many activities. Done with my independence, my freedom of movement. I was nineteen. The doctor's diagnosis was bad news: I was suffering from the life-ending illness ALS and did not have much longer to live. I was crushed. I could only despair. My whole world fell apart. I had to give up one thing after another. I lost everything that was dear to me. It was hell. Go stand where there is no place to stand. Well, now, for me there was no longer any place to go stand at all!

Nevertheless, there was something in me that did not want to give up. Maybe it was just stubbornness—I'm a very stubborn person. I wanted to search, even though I did not know where or what. Hisamatsu's phrase "Go stand where there is no place to stand," could drive me wild. Now I say: these words express something incredibly profound. I even dare say that there's no other way.

Two years long I searched for a way out of my despair. Nothing worked. When, however, I no longer knew where else I could look, at that low point where I had lost everything, where I thought "this is the end," "I don't see any way out," just at that impossible place with nothing to dull the pain and only the prospect of death, there opened before me—out of the blue—something of a path. And that path still opens up from time to time. But I could not hold on to it then and cannot hold on to it now, and I cannot label it. I can only say that there is something that makes me go on, right through the night . . . in tears, yes, but not broken. And that it's not an easy way.

This path revealed itself in silence. Totally by happenstance. Through a friend's initiative, I ended up at the Trappist monastery of Westvleteren. We were going to spend three days there. Before ringing the bell, my friend made the strange proposal that we would not talk to each other. Ok, agreed. We saw each other at mealtimes, we attended the liturgical prayer services, and the rest of the time we kept to ourselves. Since then I have often thought that his proposal had created an opening, an opportunity. Although at that time I felt it was weird. But I kept to it. I left him alone and passed the time by myself, in silence on a bench, just as I observed the monks did. In the year prior to this I had hit so many walls that, by way of speaking, all I could do was sit down—desperate, at the end of my rope. I was down for the count. To this day, I don't understand it in the least. I did not talk with anybody in those three days. I just sat there in silence. When I departed, my situation was as hopeless as ever but, to my and my housemates' amazement, I arrived home laughing, not understanding how or why. This experience has never left me. It was the beginning of my path with and in silence. It marks my life to this very day.

Shortly after my stay at that abbey I read the diaries of Etty Hillesum. Her words moved me. Not that I understood what she wrote about—at that time I couldn't really grasp all the things I was dealing with, they were too overpowering—but I held on to the feeling. Her words struck me particularly because of the circumstances under which they were written: the Second World War, the persecution of the Jews—a situation just as hopeless as mine. But what impressed me most was that this utter lack of hope did not destroy her. In the midst of the horror, she knew how to get to the essence of things. She arrived at love, a love so deep that she accompanied her people into the night, even though she herself could have escaped. I have always held on to that, and still do! She gave me hope that all was not lost. She kept alive in me the belief that there is a way (out), even if everything appears to lead to a "dead" end.

Years later, after spending many hours of quiet time, I began to understand the value and the truth of her words—pointing to a path of silence, just as in Zen. Etty writes somewhere that thinking never quite does it. I found that unimaginable and shocking. At the time I was studying at the University of Leuven and I lived completely in my head. Not to approach things with your mind was inconceivable. But if all you have left is tears, thinking doesn't do much for you. When I fell ill I thought and read until I was groggy with fatigue, searching for meaning. I had to and would find an answer. And then you read, from an intelligent woman, that this is not the way, "that you can never think your way out of difficult emotional states. That then something else has to happen. That you have to become passive and that you have to listen. That you have to reconnect with a bit of eternity." And also: "That another person cannot help you. That you have to listen to what is inside you." Etty Hillesum has a beautiful word for it: *hineinhorchen*. To listen within, and there "to wait until you become one big space inside, without the sneaky bushes that obstruct the view. So that in this way something of God enters into you. To wait until something wants to melt and wants to start flowing in you."

This mysterious, indefinable way with and in silence is what I want to deal with in this book. About my struggle with a situation without prospect but also about *hineinhorchen* and listening to what is within. Because the words of Etty Hillesum, together with the silence in that abbey, definitively led me into another direction, and there is no going back. I no longer look for answers. I only look for silence. Silence allows something wonderful to be born. The way of silence is, however, also a tough and difficult path. Hopeless misery remains hopeless misery, a wall remains a wall, and living with that is no laughing matter. And yet, there *is* something else. I simply cannot do without seeking out silence, time and again.

the spark that lives within

Night came and the illness struck me dumb.
It paralyzed my sight and my foot,
it paralyzed my sight and my foot.

The doctor came and the doctor said to me:
From this night there's no salvation,
there is no salvation.

Then Love came and Love said to me:
The night can hide your being and your roots,
but it can't hide . . . a spark.
The spark that lives within,
and that keeps on burning, despite the night.

Östen Sjöstrand

The experience that Östen Sjöstrand expresses here is also mine. An incurable, fatal disease struck me dumb and continues to do so to this day. What follows is written out of that painful experience. I realize that this is only one perspective on silence, but as I see it, it is very real. Sad to say, sometimes "to live" means to live through a merciless night. So I write first and foremost in solidarity with all those who have to battle that "night."

losing all support

In the beginning, and for a long time, I was speechless! I did not know anything anymore. There was only a scary and deadly emptiness and quiet in my head. I realized with consternation that my familiar ways of thinking, which until then had given meaning and direction to my life, lay smashed to pieces. Of course I tried to resurrect all my intellectual frames of reference, but to no avail. They lacked legs to support them. They lay in smithereens and could not be glued back together. Apparently, we can experience storms in our lives that irrevocably shatter all our convictions. Certainties are upended. Nothing provides a grip. Life itself becomes unintelligible and inhospitable. All that remains is an inscrutable night. And not for just a short while but for good.

Yet a storm like that does not just destroy. It leaves behind a pile of rubble, and to have to go on living with that is horrible. But underneath that pile of rubble something new has germinated, namely, a not-knowing. Not as a lifeless and empty notion but as something full of life, alive and kicking even! A not-knowing that becomes so fascinating that it could not be satisfied by any kind of knowing. The night can hide much . . . our being, our roots. But one thing it is unable to hide: the spark that lives in our deepest self. A spark that ignites into unknowing, and that—sometimes—burns brightly, despite the night.

It was silence that brought me to that spark. The stillness of that Trappist abbey in a far corner of Flanders. And I had the sense—because I had promptly lost the spark in the night!—that I could learn from these strange people, the monks, how to stay in contact with that spark, how I could bear my illness and the night without falling apart. For years on end, every month I sought out the quiet of that abbey for a week. I simply had to.

What is important for a monk is what he finds in his heart when all the noise of the surrounding world is silenced. There appears to be a consciousness, an understanding that can only surface when we muster the courage to accept our solitude—and to do so in a deeply silent way. A female guest at the abbey expressed it beautifully: "Dans le silence, on n'entend que l'essentiel" (In the silence, one only hears what is essential). First and foremost, the monks taught me the inestimable value of silence. To be (become) a real human being is impossible without moments of silence, without a bit of seclusion, without desert.

I learned to cultivate, to inhabit and to love my solitude. According to Rilke, a poet close to my heart, this is a real challenge—at one time he wrote to somebody: "I want to welcome, to protect, and to safeguard your solitude." I learned to be at home with myself, no matter how hard it is. It was a 180 degree turn, because I had purposefully done all I could *not* to feel this solitude, to escape it.

More than anything, I learned patience. With their attitude of waking and waiting, monks embody better than anyone else the beautiful but difficult words of Simone Weil: "What is most important cannot be searched for, it must be awaited." Psalm 27, which they sing every Tuesday evening prior to entering into the stillness of the night, expresses this very nicely: "Wait for the Lord; be strong, and let your heart take courage; wait for the Lord."

deeply human feelings

Now that I have used the word psalm, I have to mention a second idiosyncrasy of the Western monastic tradition that left a deep impression: the central place of the psalms. The monks sing the psalms, all one hundred and fifty of them, over the span of two weeks. In the fourth century AD, the Egyptian desert hermits actually prayed them all every single day. By heart, if you please. The psalms power the Benedictine tradition! By singing them so frequently, the texts continue to resound in the mind throughout the day, just like a tune that's impossible to get out of your head. They bubble up all the time and move the heart toward what is essential. I experienced this myself as a blessing and a treasure during the year that I lived with the Benedictine sisters of Saint Lioba.

Bible scholars often consider the psalms a difficult genre because poetic expression is foreign to our culture. Nevertheless, the psalms have touched me to the core. I recognized myself in these ancient texts. That is, I think, because they give expression to all feelings that are profoundly human, from gratitude and emotion to disenchantment, envy, hatred, fear, sorrow, and even unbelief.

The psalms don't shy away from reality. They don't avoid life's many contradictions but, on the contrary, they engage precisely in the tensions that exist between them. By falling and by getting up, by loving and by cursing. Life's delights are serenaded extensively, its burdens are not suppressed. For example, they can say in one breath: "You are gods, all of you sons of the Most High" and "yet like men you shall die." Similarly, while there is no more heartfelt cry for justice than found in the psalms, at the same time they teem with murderous thoughts and injustices.

I have always thought it profoundly wise that the monks insist on singing the whole book, including the parts that won't do. For example, how can you pray: "A blessing on anyone who seizes your babies/and shatters them against a rock!" "That's not Christian," is our spontaneous response. Benoît Standaert, a monk at the abbey of Zevenkerken near Bruges, once told me, however: "Teach your mouth to say what resides in your heart." Well, the psalms teach you that. They challenge us to humility. Everything that resides in our heart stands exposed and naked. There is a good amount of cursing. There is an explicit recognition of negative feelings. Reciting those texts, your own darkness rises to the surface, and that is liberating. When as a girl of nineteen I saw my whole future go up in smoke, the psalms saved me.

interconnectedness

To sing the psalms gives expression to a worldwide interconnectedness. They are songs that create in the singer a surprising, paradoxical dynamic of "being pulled *into* and *out of* oneself."

At one time we recited the whole book aloud with a group of forty people, in a soft murmuring voice with each person doing about four psalms. Gradually the murmur became quieter . . . until only three, only two voices were heard, and then only one . . . to end with an impressive silence. Our minds had seen the whole world. For in the psalms the complete history of Israel is preserved as in a nutshell, and within this tumultuous history the whole spectrum of human happiness and sorrow is displayed. When you've gone through the whole book, the complete human condition has passed in review. The psalms strengthen us; they are a living expression of the solidarity that awakens in us when we dare to assume our solitude and vulnerability. The deepest solidarity, with *each* of our fellow human beings, no matter where, no matter who.

Further, the psalms have moved me so because they, just like the poems and songs of Huub Oosterhuis, are addressed directly to God without specifying who or what that God exactly is. What a relief in a church that mainly talks *about* God! I picked up a very different notion from the monks. Namely, that talking about God is a fiction, an illusion, the result of a blind spot, a presumption, whether conscious or not. That God can never be an object of our thinking or speaking. That if we want to deal with the living God, we have to resist that temptation once and for all.

deeper silence

A few years ago I learned a completely different way of living in silence, the way of Zen Buddhism. But, actually, completely different? No: for me they are two expressions of the inner path, and there are more. Western tradition, with its extensive liturgy, is muscularly verbal. Zen Buddhism, in my understanding, is not and engages in a deeper silence. But I cannot and do not want to play them off against each other.

The power of the Benedictine tradition is that it's verbal. The power of the Zen tradition is that it's not. They differ significantly, but on the inside they are closer than the outside would make you think.

Nevertheless, the way of Zen, as I got to know it with the Maha Karuna Ch'an, speaks to me possibly more forcefully. Nowhere have I experienced such an intensity of silence! In Christian churches there is—in the best case—silence after the Word. In Zen meditation silence prevails and a word rises up out of the silence only rarely. Unimaginable how much more profoundly penetrating a word can be after you've been silent all day!

The soberness of it all appeals to me. It is simplicity itself. It lacks any kind of pretense. It is accessible to everybody. Moreover, it is easy to combine with living in society, while it's a whole lot more difficult to go and memorize the psalms on your own. And if you don't know the psalms by heart, you lose the major part of their dynamism and power.

But Zen is especially attractive to me because it is a way of "un-imagining" *par excellence*. The night has brought me to a point where images no longer work, so much so that I can barely stand them. You can reach a point in life in which you are facing suffering in all its rawness to such an extent that all your constructs (including images of God)—no matter how true and well-intended—appear stacked on a slippery slope, deserving only a good kick, that you have run out of answers and that you cannot stand to be fed any more, that you no longer find meaning in anything, that all you can do is shut up. Or curse and weep, like Job.

kicking metaphors

Sylvie Germain, a contemporary of mine, wrote an impressive piece about this topic in her book *The Echos of Silence* [*Les échos du silence*]. Contemplating the savagery of the last century, she is exasperated with the Christian metaphors she grew up with. They don't make sense. They don't do anything for her. The only thing she can do is kick them. She no longer can figure it out. And yet she does not succumb to nihilism. No, she maintains the sense *and* nonsense of life in one enormous, almost superhuman arc of tension. She does not lose sight of the nonsense for one minute, but she also does not let go of the sense of life. She does something odd: she goes and positions herself right in the middle of the painful place of "no answers," and from there, from this nowhere, numbed by night and abandonment, she ventures on an odyssey . . . an adventure into the mystery of silence itself.

She writes:

> We must take the risk of following a path that accords with silence, without requiring that the silence ever be broken and without putting an end to it with an irrevocable emptiness. A path of mere drifting through the ever-expanding desert that is silence itself. And, just like the miserable Job, all the while we "take our flesh between our teeth," and our whole being lies exposed in the palms of our hands. There are mental plains that are so arid, shorn so bare, so desolate, that we can only enter upon them if we are ready to place our thoughts "outside the ego" and allow the dike of reason to collapse, so as to deliver our spirit up to the unknown, the unforeseeable. All righteous men and women and all saints who have suffered the night of emptiness from beginning to end, and who against all adversity still stood tall in their faith, carried themselves like this: as nomads of silence, emptied from the ground to the rooftop, as guardians of the void, of the unthinkable. As men following a divining rod, searching for the source of unsuspected meaning.

If, when face to face with the horror of the night, a path can still be found, then it is one of and in silence, and there can be no other! I do not believe in metaphors and theories, nor in answers and opinions, I only believe in the question, the story, the smile, the cry, and the silence.

left to find my own way

I'll never forget my first day of Zen at the Harp in Izegem. No speeches. No prolonged reflections. Just an extremely brief explanation, after which I was warmly invited to join and sit in the silence. It struck me that I was left to find my own way right from the start. Similarly, I was struck when I started reading about it that Zen is not a theory, not a philosophy, that there is no dogma, no method even, but simply: a direct engagement with the Mystery in a mindful presence, without wanting to grasp that Mystery.

I am very impressed by the fact that certain intuitions, which I also found in Christian mystics like John of the Cross, constitute the essence of Zen Buddhism, whereas in the church they are tolerated only at the margin. For example, the sense that, at bottom, happiness consists in going beyond our ego, which leads to a profound reverence for everything that exists. Or the impasse presented by Ulrich Libbrecht in his book *Is God Dead?* [*Is God dood?*]: "Every theory about nirvana is nonsense, because it tries to express that which cannot be spoken; but also all action to achieve nirvana is nonsense. It is an impasse: one wants to achieve something, but one can neither think about it nor take action . . . In sum, one can only prepare the terrain, create the space, but one cannot oblige the light to come and to shine upon it."

Maybe this time the Buddhists are the missionaries! Not to teach us ideas about God but rather to help us unlearn them. But then we in the West would have to accept first that we need conversion. In any case, this way of being with and in silence brings me to what, to my sense, must have animated Jesus: an enormous respect for the living reality of God, right here among us, ungraspable, unspeakably close; and how that deepest reality loosens in us a flowing current, a compassion, that runs to everything and everybody. A respect that must have touched him so deeply that he continued to have faith, against all odds, even when in his despair and misery he could only cry: "My God, my God, why have You forsaken me?"

I note that Buddhism is also expressed in a verbal tradition, by way of sutras and *koans.* I don't dare to say much about that. I have not lived with and in it sufficiently! But long enough to feel that these are texts by which I want to allow myself to be re-formed, just as the psalms have done. Long enough also to be struck by the sense of paradox that many of these texts imply, such as in the powerful phrase of Hisamatsu: "Exactly here and now, when nothing works, what are you going to do?"

To me, paradoxes are essential. Actually, these days I can only tolerate thoughts that are pregnant with paradox. Because suffering challenges us to live mutually exclusive truths at the same time. I marvel at the fact that I can find myself so fortified and so understood by words from a totally different culture. It is, I think, because paradox is its warp and woof. "The truth of paradoxes," writes Benoît Standaert, "of course never belongs to a closed club. It is apparent also to others, the so-called outsiders."

open hands

To conclude, I would like to join the French psychoanalyst Marie Balmary in a heartfelt plea "to keep the gates of heaven (whatever that may mean) wide open." She believes that the intensity and the freedom of our life depend on whether or not the space above us is open or closed, just like a fire in the hearth depends on an open and well-venting chimney.

When I encountered the Western contemplative tradition, it unlocked and opened something in me. The fire could and can burn. I could breathe again. To live, I must have that opening to another side that is beyond my grasp. But open means open. I cannot stand having that open space filled up. It must remain empty but open . . . That's why I think there is no stronger chimney than meditating in pure silence. Simone Weil—my apology for yet another reference to her, she made such a deep impression on me—puts it like this:

"The most important thing is that our thinking be empty, expectant, without being on the lookout for something specific, while being open to receive in its naked truth that what is to enter."

How it works, I don't know. The important thing, I believe, is to connect with a path and to go.

I want to end the way I started: with a poem. Because, of course, the fire also flares in places other than abbeys of Christian and Buddhist monks!

None can I tell it plain,
none will believe,
nor can I just explain,
only indicate can I, and warily,
with much detour, and quandary,
what thought alone cannot achieve.
So severely it indebted me
that it took without the slightest pity:
my hands, my eyes, my words,
henceforward all became so insufficient
all that I saw or heard,
all in which I had been so proficient,
this all has left me, piece by piece.
My words no longer fit,
except to whisper: peace, peace.
Surely God will gather it
somewhere, in you, in me.
The rest I need not see.

Gabriël Smit

light without form

Strain to enter
into the treasure chamber's cell
that lies within you,
and there you will see
what treasure is stored in heaven.

Isaac the Syrian

All things considered, I came to the Christian faith in a curious way. I realize that I came upon the treasures of Christianity through a strange door. A little back door, actually. Half decayed, hidden under a thick layer of dust, barely known and noticed. But on the inside, jumping with life. You see, I got to know the Christian faith through its contemplative form, through abbeys. This is no faith of rules and merits. Neither is it a faith of dogmas that must be accepted as truths. Here I discovered a faith of lived experience and inwardness, preserved throughout the centuries and passed on. Only later did I come to understand how exceptional my approach had been.

It was kind of crazy. I had not attended Mass in years. I knew nothing about abbeys. I had even less of a sense of what can happen to you in silence. Student life—yes, that I knew. And I knew that in a quiet moment, negative thoughts can surprise you. But that at times silence can fill a person with unspeakable richness—no, that was new and foreign to me. I could not figure it out. But it exerted an irresistible pull, and I returned.

Later, in the guest library of the abbey of Westvleteren, I came upon a book by a monk, and I started reading. I tried to understand what had happened to me. The manner in which that monk expressed his faith hit home. According to him, fundamentally, it's about an *experience* of a dying—and that dying can be to anything—that unexpectedly tilts to life. He talked constantly about "bumping against the limits of our human capabilities," and that we had to reach that frontier finally "to tumble into God." Not the God beyond or above us but the God who lives—wonder of wonders—in our deepest self. "Toppling over into inwardness," he also called it. It was moving to read that sooner or later we all come face to face with our fundamental poverty and loneliness. It's a painful moment. But in the eyes of this monk it's also the opportunity to discover that inner balm. Even more so, it's how we become truly human. In that toppling over we land on a point of unexpected freedom—a universal interconnectedness opens up.

I never had expected that this is what Christianity is all about. For me, faith was a collection of notions that did not begin to make sense. For that monk it was different. I identified with what he put into words. It expressed exactly what I had experienced. When I had arrived at the abbey of Westvleteren on a warm summer day, I was at the end of my rope. I had tried literally everything to escape the dead end I found myself in. Without success. The ALS diagnosis had robbed me of my future, and I had been incapable of doing anything about it. To bump up against the limits of your human capabilities . . . I had experienced it firsthand! And all of a sudden, I toppled over, into something entirely different. I understood what that monk meant with "a dying that, to your own astonishment, tumbles toward life." Just like that. In the silence. In the midst of death. Without any personal effort. Indeed, something like an anointing. Deep inside, where you least expected it. And that makes you a whole other human being and causes you to look at life completely differently, even if it is still you. This became the ground upon which I came to understand and to practice Christianity. Later, after having had arguments with people, I realized how far removed this perspective is from the usual vision of faith. This monk's perspective apparently was out of the ordinary. But for me it was a door. I probably never would have entered through any other.

Years later I had the opportunity to interview that monk. His name is André Louf, his book that so impressed me called *Tuning In to Grace*. Louf regrets the ossification of abstract ideas that causes us to lose sight of the fact that the Christian experience possesses a fundamental *inward* character. As a matter of fact, he claims that every person, from whatever culture or religion, can achieve the same inner experience. The Bible repeats constantly that each person has an inner dwelling: he is the temple of God (1 Cor 3, 16). Alas! Most of us are unaware of this hidden inner treasure, even if we are believers. Louf did not come across as a softy but as a man with guts. He used strong language—for example, that every contemplative sooner or later becomes an expert in atheism.

So I engaged the old monk in conversation, and what transpired? He owes all his depth to a Syrian monk of the seventh century: Isaac the Syrian or Isaac of Nineveh. What I like about Louf and these Syrian monks is their searching, groping language. Their manner of thinking comes close to experiencing. These monks apparently don't have much confidence in reason and ideas. Rationalization can be a dramatic mistake in theology, and the monks stay well clear of it. They prefer to keep the unnamable unnamed. For them language is an instrument for inquiry, and it cannot be held in a vise. Because sooner or later you confront the Mystery, and you have to let go of every notion you know. What is important for them is to grow . . . from the outside to the inside and from inside until they track the "Light without form." This sounds very different from the faith of my upbringing that did nothing for me. But it is also Christianity. Even if it is only a tiny branch of the river. Has it not always been like this? Is it not true that words that originally reflected a lived experience time and again become ossified, dead notions that don't communicate anything?

Isaac the Syrian appears to have influenced Dostoevsky and Russian spirituality generally. He was even read as far as Japan. And every person who reads him is delighted. I am not surprised. The most important discovery in this life lives everywhere. Whoever has touched this Light without form recognizes it immediately, regardless of the manner in which it is described or put into song. Always and everywhere there have been people who suddenly took a tumble, and in that fall something akin to a marvelous treasure chamber opened up in their heart. You can call it anointment by the Spirit, Light without form, original countenance, Buddha nature, or something else. Words are relative. They are humble attempts to say something about that indefinable, that unnamable that is born in silence: Love, from inside out and open. For everything and everybody. There is a depth where everything comes together or, maybe, from where everything actually begins.

It strikes me that novelists also speak, albeit falteringly, about this treasure room in the heart. I like novels. It's a genre that stays close to life as it is lived and does not lend itself to rationalization. Novelists often bear probing witness to this Light without form. I am thinking of a passage by the Nigerian writer Ben Okri in his novel *Astonishing the Gods*. It's about a man who is engaged in some kind of struggle with death, and who, to his surprise, tumbles toward the most brilliant light.

Okri writes:

> At that point his mind plunged into total darkness. He felt himself spinning in that darkness. Then he felt himself falling, falling away from himself, falling without end into a darkness that got deeper and more unbearable. The only thing he could do to rescue himself from the

sheer terror of his internal abyss was to scream. He screamed in absolute horror of becoming more invisible than he already was. So loud and so piercingly did he scream that the entire island seemed to resound with it. After a while he wasn't sure if it was him or if it was the universe that was screaming. He felt himself falling through layers of the world's unheard agony. And when he stopped screaming, he stopped falling. And when he opened his eyes he found himself bathed in the most splendid black starlight. And up above, like a forgotten god of the mountains, a towering colossus made of primal light, was the startling presence of the great archangel of invisibility.

One moment she was there; the next moment she was gone. Her presence was so brief that it seemed a lightning flash of eternity had passed through him. When the great archangel disappeared, leaving a glorious intensity of lights in the giant spaces she had occupied, with her wing span alone seeming to cover the entire island, he felt that he too had become completely insubstantial, and mightier. He was not sure how, or in what way.

"I don't understand anything at all," he said to the wind.

"Don't try to understand," the voice, his guide, said to him. "Understanding comes beyond trying. It comes from beyond."

"Beyond where?"

The voice stayed silent.

I think of the book *With Open Eyes*, a conversation with Marguerite Yourcenar. She also deals with a wonderful balm from inside out. Somewhere in the interview, Yourcenar says: "Undeniably, there exists a paradise of the heart, a bliss experienced by the mind, or the soul, or even the body, when they are freed of nearly all uselessness, and for some people that bliss, which escapes definition, inexplicably stays intact in the midst of despair about suffering in the world, and for this also no words exist." This is language close to the experience. The only language I trust. Searching, groping, without wanting to grasp. Yourcenar and Okri express themselves very differently from Isaac the Syrian. But they give witness to the same lived experience. They also try to talk about a hidden treasure room, an intangible Light without form, at the bottom of one's heart.

I have a friend who is a sculptor. A while ago she participated in an exhibition at Talbot House in Poperinge, a house where English and Irish soldiers could briefly escape the horrors of World War I. The exhibition's theme: *resilience*. She asked me to say something at the opening. On such occasions I always tend to borrow from novelists, because they deal squarely with terror *and* hope without diminishing the lived experience. I chose the words of Marguerite Yourcenar. I also referenced the moving novel *A Long Long Way* by Irish writer Sebastian Barry, about the ups and downs of Irish soldiers in the trenches of 1914–1918. Even there, to my amazement, I bumped fleetingly into this intangible Light without form.

Barry's book opens with a sweet scene. In Dublin a little boy is born, Willie Dunne, like a snippet of a song, a point of light in the snowy darkness, a beginning . . . But immediately the tone turns:

> And all those boys of Europe born in those times, Russian, French, Belgian, Serbian, Irish, English, Scottish, Welsh, Italian, Prussian, German, Austrian, Turkish—and Canadian, Australian, American, Zulu, Gurkha, Cossack, and all the rest—their fate was written in a ferocious chapter of the book of life, certainly. Those millions of mothers and their million gallons of mothers' milk, millions of instances of small-talk and baby-talk, beatings and kisses, ganseys and shoes, piled up in history in great ruined heaps, with a loud and broken music, human stories told for nothing, for ashes, for death's amusement, flung on the mighty scrapheap of

> souls, all those million boys in all their humours to be milled by the mill-stones of a coming war.

Barry's novel follows the adventures of Willie Dunne until he is killed in action. This rock-hard book takes the reader to a hellish no-man's-land, where the madness of war can be felt—but can no longer be expressed in words. Yet even so, in certain moments, very briefly, in these soldiers: that resilience, that strange bliss, that inner balm of which Yourcenar, Okri, the monks, and so many others try to speak. When they are singing together, when they are thinking about their sweethearts, when Father Buckley speaks words of encouragement, when in a quiet moment they stick their heads out of the trenches and see the immaculate, flat land . . . Yes, even there, existed a strange Light without form. And yes, even there existed a paradise of the heart. Undeniably.

new year's wish

We all live
to discover beauty.
Everything else is a kind
of waiting.

Kahlil Gibran

Christmas vacation. There is a sharp frost. But for the exhibit *Buddha's Smile* in Brussels we brave the cold with pleasure. After all, you don't have the opportunity to see masterpieces of Buddhist art every day. I'll never get to Seoul. I gladly put up with taking the train to Brussels, even though it's frigid.

After the exhibit we stroll through the charmingly illuminated streets of Brussels. We walk along the Grand Market Place, the Kleine Zavel Square . . . Suddenly, the glacial wind is blowing us straight in the face. With difficulty we make our way back, against the current of visitors, to the market place decorated for Christmas, to the central station. When we get there we find out that we're early. Another half hour before the next train to Kortrijk. We decide to stay in the train station and to seek refuge in the warmth of the waiting room. Except for a few seats in the corner on the left side, the hall is absolutely packed. I march straight away to the left corner and drop in one of the empty chairs. Instantaneously my nostrils are assaulted by a sickening smell. Just as if somebody had piddled and left without cleaning up the mess. That's nice, I think. I look around to figure out what is causing this stench, and then I realize with a start that it's the woman beside me. I realize right away why these chairs were empty.

The woman looks neglected. With wide gestures she turns the pages of something that once was a magazine. She halts occasionally. Not to read. But to scribble on the page until it's full. As if her life depended on it. I see two ripped plastic bags at her feet. My first impulse: stand up and get out of here. The stench is impossible. But then I think: you can't do this. Maybe that sounds crazy, because the woman was so far gone as to preclude any real contact. Yet I did not want to get up. Staying put was an expression—no matter how small—of "not avoiding the contact."

All of a sudden, the woman asks me what time it is. "I'm waiting for somebody," she adds by way of explanation. She barely finishes speaking when two inspectors appear in the waiting room: "Tickets please!" I saw right away that their appearance had only one purpose: to remove the woman. Yes, indeed: "Does the lady in the corner there have a ticket please?" No answer. "Ma'am, your ticket please?" She protests gently, "I'm waiting for somebody." The two men exchange a meaningful glance: "You have been waiting here for hours already. You sat here waiting yesterday. Come on, outside!" The woman rises, gathers all her possessions in her two hands, and disappears. Outside only the glacial cold awaits. Nobody stops her. Nobody stands up for her. Not me either. These are the kind of moments when you're ashamed of your lack of humanity, your failure of courage.

Christmas vacation. Time for New Year's wishes. No matter how nice and meaningful these reciprocal greetings may be, something does not go over well with me. I discussed it today with the physical therapist. He had read me the wishes he was going to send out. On top of the list, good health. Then, satisfaction at work. And of course, happiness with the children and the family. Optimism. It looks dry in my summary. His version was much more entertaining, and the enthusiasm with which he recited his verses made me smile. Yet it bothered me. A feeling that often happens to me with New Year's wishes.

It made me think of the homeless woman of yesterday. What good are all these wishes to her? I was reminded of the movie we had watched the night before. *Babel.* By Alejandro Gonzáles Iñárritu. The movies of this Mexican director always deal with a singular event from the standpoint of the various people involved. Same thing with this one. An American woman traveling through the Moroccan desert with her husband is accidentally shot by two children trying out their dad's rifle. A deaf-mute girl from Tokyo desperately tries to attract the attention of some men. And a Mexican au pair who resides illegally in the United States gets into trouble with the US border patrol. The movie zips from one continent to another until you hold so many pieces of the puzzle in your hands that you can readily complete it. But while you're pleasantly busy puzzling, the uncomfortable feeling creeps into your gut that there is misery in every life. Sometimes things turn out well. At least for the time being. Sometimes things turn out badly. As for example for the deaf-mute Japanese girl who must swallow rejection after rejection. The movie ends in Tokyo. The girl stands on the balcony of her parents' apartment: naked, surrounded by a city of millions, yet all alone.

I put the following question to my physical therapist: what are all our wishes actually worth? They are beautiful things, albeit fragile and transitory, every single one. Some people get to enjoy this fragile happiness for a while. Others keep missing it. It appears to me that a wish is only worthwhile if it applies to *everybody*, without exception. I mean it. You only have to suffer some mishap, and a lot of these New Year's wishes sound hollow. Every year I have to hear it again: "Good health. That's the most important thing." But are these words not exasperating if, health-wise, things can only go downhill for you? Somebody wrote me once at New Year's:

"I know that your life is a mess, and that is awful. Yet even on the biggest mess, flowers are sure to grow again one day." I was moved. A good friend who worked for a while at a center for asylum seekers wished the people there a happy New Year with this beautiful phrase: "Wherever you go, whatever you do, may at least one dream come true." That also moved me deeply. But it is still not a wish that is applicable to everyone.

On the inside flap of the book jacket for *More Than Anyone Can Do: Zen Talks* appears the following: "It's about the deep desire and the simultaneous certainty that nothing and nobody is left behind." I received these Zen talks by Ton Lathouwers after two days' meditation at the Harp in Izegem. That had been my first contact with Zen. Bull's eye, right away. It has stayed with me forever. The Zen perspective that *everything* will be saved, even already *is* saved, including the last pebble, moved me deeply. There exists a grace from which nobody is excluded. Now that's a New Year's wish! The only one we should be allowed to send. Kahlil Gibran expresses the same longing and the same certainty: "All of us live to discover beauty." But that saving grace and that beauty don't just appear out of nowhere. They have everything to do, in a noncausative way, with one's commitment to them. That also hit me. It was a revelation. "No matter how numerous the living beings are, *I* vow to liberate them all," says the first Commitment of the Bodhisattva. Thus it also depends on me, no matter how crazy and impossible that may appear. Does the longing *live* in me that nobody be left behind? Or could I not care less?

Stef Renodeyn writes in the introduction to his photography book *The Person that I Am* [*De mens die ik ben*]: "To look the broken person in the face is a first step in showing humanity." This artist-photographer centered his artistic focus on people living at the margins of society. For five years, he looked for beggars, addicts, and homeless people in the city of Antwerp. He spent time with them. He tried to get to know their lives. With their consent, he photographed them in their usual environment. *The Person that I Am* depicts this group without voyeurism and without the usual stereotyping. The images emphasize the importance of the diversity and the uniqueness of these men and women. It's why the book includes their names. "These people may be failures from the standpoint of society, but as people they never are, for the simple reason that they exist," says the artist. Taking pictures is his way of picking people up from the street. It's his way of expressing that deep desire. *The Person that I Am* is living testimony to the first Commitment of the Bodhisattva because it requires courage to look these individuals in the eye. It's not easy. We have to wrestle our way through a confrontation with ourselves.

In Chinese Buddhism, this deep longing and simultaneous certainty that nobody will be left behind is symbolized by a womanly figure, expressing infinite compassion: Kwan Yin. She descends to the deepest depth of hell to save everybody, without exception. To that end she is even prepared to sacrifice her own salvation. I was surprised to read in *More Than Anyone Can Do* that Dostoevsky most likely was inspired by this Buddhist Bodhisattva of infinite compassion when he was writing his novel *The Brothers Karamazov*. For psychologists there is a lot to chew on in the novels of Dostoevsky and, naturally, *The Brothers Karamazov* is one of my favorite books. But that kind of depth I had missed in my reading of it.

At the beginning of the "The Grand Inquisitor" in *The Brothers Karamazov*, Dostoevsky has the character Ivan talk about an ancient Russian legend called *The Mother of God Visits the Torments*. Referring to a particularly pitiful group of sinners in hell, the ancient legend says "these God forgets." But there is one person who does not forget them: the Mother of God. In the end, she obtains that the torments of hell cease every year from Good Friday to Pentecost. During that time all the damned may participate in the heavenly glory of God's elect. Ton Lathouwers writes the following about this episode: "Our first reaction is probably: 'A rather poor outcome. She should not have been satisfied with that.' That is true," he says, "but then the story would have been robbed of its deepest significance. Because it is not about the Bodhisattva or the Mother of God doing it alone, as a power outside and beyond us. That would be too easy. As a lonely protagonist, she takes a step through which the impossible becomes possible with respect to the most agonizing and fundamental problem of existence: the salvation of *all without distinction*. After that it's up to us, each one of us, silent and alone, to take that step, no matter how impossible it may seem."

To clarify the essence of Zen, Ton Lathouwers also refers, to my surprise, to a story from the Old Testament: Moses who climbs Mount Sinai to encounter Yahweh. In that meeting, Yahweh complains about his nation. He tells Moses about his intention to destroy them and to save only Moses and his descendants. But Moses unconditionally defends his people. The dialogue reaches its climax with the following words, which must have filled Moses with horror but he spoke them nevertheless: "If You do not agree, You can also forget me. Cross out, then, also my name from the Book of Life." My first contact with Zen led me right away to the core of the religion in which, as a Westerner, I had been brought up. Stronger still: the deep silence of Zen and this handful of *teishos* revealed the biblical tradition in an entirely new way. It surprised me. But perhaps it's not so strange. Does what is essential not shine through everywhere . . . in east and west, north and south, through me, through you?

Christianity also possesses impressive texts that express the deep longing for redemption of every person and every thing. I am thinking of Huub Oosterhuis's beautiful song *Larger than Our Heart* [*Groter dan ons hart*]:

You who are love, deep as the sea,
streaking as lightning, stronger than death,
do not allow one child to be lost.
You who forgets no name and scorns no one—
do not allow death to divide and empty everything,
don't let us die the second death.
For all those who are crucified,
do not be nobody,
be their future unseen.
For those who feel by you deserted,
for all who cannot bear their fate,
for those who are defenseless
at the hands of people.
For those among us who share your name:
refugees, strangers, do not be nobody.
(. . .)
As a deer longs for living water,
make us yearn for the day
that we, a divided people still,
are gathered in your city,
in you united and complete,
in you forever more.

"I'm waiting for somebody," said the homeless woman in the Brussels-Central train station. Even though nobody had come that day. Nor the day before. It surely was not a matter of naiveté on her part. Were her words a lame excuse? A story with which she hoped to prolong her time in the heated hall? Ostensibly, yes. But as far as I'm concerned, her words also evince an extraordinary depth and power. A stubborn hope resonates in them, despite everything else. "I'm waiting for somebody." I did not find it crazy at all for the woman to say that. Even if I have no clue *how* her waiting will be answered, this I know for sure: that woman does not wait in vain.

out of boredom

The door of happiness opens
to the inside.

Kierkegaard

One overcast Sunday afternoon, bored by the fact that I have to write an article about boredom, I sit at my computer. The writing doesn't flow, and to amuse myself I decide to Google my subject. My search yields 432,000 results: "Boredom—telephone use by children and adolescents," "Boredom at the office," "Join Clan against Boredom on Netlog," etc. Boredom appears to be an issue on the Internet. Meanwhile, over a cup of coffee, my husband, who teaches high school, tells me that one of the words in the top ten of the youth vocabulary is *dull.* "And it has nothing to do with my teaching style!" he adds impishly. "They become bored real quick, and then they become bores themselves." He laughs, while I move back to the computer to continue my writing.

In any event, boredom is certainly an issue in my life. Nothing is so tedious as not being able to get around. If you depend on others for everything, the space to do (fun) things becomes very small. Because of my illness I often feel condemned to a living space that is literally not larger than the square meter of my existence. I look like one of these crazy monks who spend years sitting on a pole. My life is terribly monotonous.

In the morning a nurse helps me to get out of bed and get dressed. When she leaves, somebody else is already waiting to help with breakfast. The whole morning is devoted to physical therapy (passive and active movement, pain therapy, stretching, etc.). In the afternoon I'm free. But that's not saying a lot when you basically can't use your arms. Fortunately, I have an assistive computer system and my arms allow just enough movement to enable me to read. But I have to pace myself carefully. It doesn't take much for me to need a rest. If your only freedom of movement consists of moving between your computer and your chair, with once in a while a short detour via the meditation mat, you get fed up with it pretty quickly. Talk about monotony.

Currently I am enjoying a public assistance benefit that allows me to hire extra help, which opens up a bit more room for living. Once in a while I can even take on a challenge like providing counseling or giving a lecture. I enjoy that. I don't want to diminish the value of a positive challenge by any means. I have suffered more than anybody from the absence of a challenge. Yet, in comparison with others, my life is and remains monotonous and boring. My room to live may have expanded a bit beyond a pole thanks to the public assistance benefit, but life keeps me on a short leash. As a result, I spend a good deal of my time "sitting on a pole," bored stiff.

For a long time I thought that utter boredom will kill you. But more and more I find myself rethinking that. Maybe we should not avoid boredom at all cost. Maybe it has something to tell us. In the beginning I fought boredom with all my might, but to no avail. Getting in touch with the Trappists of Westvleteren, however, started me thinking differently. There I saw people leading extremely dull and monotonous lives. They spent many hours in silence, yet they radiated happiness. I thought: If they don't die of boredom, then all cannot be lost for me. The radiance in their eyes fascinated me. It was more than I could understand. I saw them regularly sitting quietly on a bench, and I started doing the same thing, no matter how boring it was. It's an attitude that touched me deeply, and that I experienced again later with the practice of Zen.

For a long time I lived with the idea that my illness was at fault, and that healthy, active people are spared this kind of boredom. But I'm also rethinking that. I'm getting on to forty, and I see people of my age struggling with various forms of boredom, just like me. From a psychological perspective it is in midlife that we sense for the first time the relativity of all that (we think) we are, taste, know, possess. Boredom hits. The older we get, the harder it is. It's as if we need to make a choice every time it happens: to try to make the boredom go away with "busy, busy, busy" and new gadget after new gadget, or to confront the boredom head-on, hoping for the best.

Another person who thinks that abundance, and our ability freely to move among a great multiplicity of things, does not preserve us from boredom, is Awee Prins. Among the 432,000 Google results for boredom, I came upon an interview with him in connection with his book *Out of Boredom* [*Uit verveling*]. According to this philosopher from Rotterdam, boredom is a fundamental, but hidden, attitude of our time. So I hang out a bit with Awee Prins, and no matter how strange this sounds, on a rainy Sunday afternoon I'm getting captivated by the subject of boredom.

In an interview with the newspaper *Loyalty* [*Trouw*], Prins expresses himself with verve. He posits that those who add to prosperity, add to boredom. Indeed, it seems that the more things you own, the less important they become, and eventually they become meaningless. People in the West have so much readily available these days. But there is little that actually moves them. We are continually on the lookout for what is interesting and for what we think will keep boredom at bay. And although we can keep this up for years, rather successfully, boredom remains a threat. It lies in wait around almost every corner. We always try to beat it; if we fail, boredom hits us like a rock.

Prins tries to explain this. Maybe happiness does not consist so much in what is *interesting* in people and things. Happiness has to do with *taking an interest* in people and things. Interest as *inter-esse*, from the Latin verb "*to be among*" people and things. But there is not much *inter-esse* going on anymore, says Prins. We do not find ourselves actually in the midst of living reality anymore. This has to do with the fact that we have difficulty concentrating and that our patience runs short.

To the question of whether he sees a way out of boredom, Prins replies that he does not believe in Fukuyama's smart drugs. To his mind, boredom is not purely a physiological problem but rather an existential one. He appears not to have any faith in our restless busy-ness and hedonistic culture. In what does he believe? In adopting a different attitude: an attitude in which boredom is accepted. "We must have patience with things," he says. "I believe in lingering with things. By always avoiding boredom we never reach what 'deep boredom' can teach us."

It's absolutely amazing how Awee Prins arrives at the same conclusion as me, he by way of abundance, me by way of monotony: we cannot escape boredom and, rather than frenetically chasing it away, we must dare to accept it. His words remind me of the *koan*: "How do you put a step forward from the top of a pole one hundred meters high?" Just like the Trappists, Awee Prins seems to say: very simple. By going to sit on that pole of boredom . . . Just like these crazy monks? Yes. These crazy monks are not really all that crazy!

What also strikes me as right in his argument is that the essence of boredom has to do with meaninglessness. Monotony and abundance are not boring in themselves. But the meaninglessness of monotony is and so is the meaninglessness of abundance. Fullness of meaning has to do with relationship, with wanting to be connected. It comes from *inter-esse*, from being among people and things—in one word, from being involved. How do we achieve *inter-esse*? Prins expresses it with a beautiful image: we have to learn to walk more slowly from one place to the next. If you move slowly, you wander among things (*inter-esse*), you see things, and they become captivating. If you drive fast, you fly past everything, you miss what surrounds you, and the drive becomes a bore. "Are we there yet?"

At one point the interview touches on meditation techniques. Prins says that they are a blessing when their purpose is contemplation. But he notes that frequently there is a typically Western strategy behind them: to be more productive. Prins believes that we often misuse Eastern philosophies. We see them as a way to bring us happiness. But as the Danish philosopher Kierkegaard has remarked, the door of happiness opens to the inside, so it doesn't matter how hard you push. Happiness comes as a bonus in a committed life. Elsewhere he says the same thing about meaning: "Meaning is not something you bestow on things, it is a bonus."

Without a life of commitment and patience, the meaning of things cannot be revealed. There is no sense pushing against that door. The only thing we can do is to live a committed life. To stay awake and to wait. Until the door opens by itself . . . I can also see another interpretation: meaning, happiness, has to do with the movement "inward." Strangely enough, the meaning of what surrounds us comes from going within. By dwelling within ourselves in stillness and attention. In that sense, we have to pull open the door to happiness ourselves after all and allow the outside to enter. We have to allow ourselves to be surprised.

Years ago, in a children's book of fewer than six pages, I came across the same insight expressed by Awee Prins in his 438-page dissertation. In 1996 that little book won the Silver Slate Pencil prize for Marit Törnqvist. The text comprises six short pieces, each abundantly illustrated. Törnqvist starts her story with the remarkable words: "On a pole somewhere in the sea sat a little girl. She sat there day and night, in good weather and in bad." Then follow four funny drawings of a little girl on a pole. You see her sitting during the day, during the night, when it snows (while she tries to catch snowflakes on the tip of her tongue), and in a stiff breeze. If that is not lingering with the things around us! I continue to marvel at the way this woman, with a children's book, could depict a way of being that so affected me when I was with Western monks, and later in Zen: sitting in silence. And sticking with the sitting. Day and night. On clear days and in storms. I once gave this children's book to the Trappists of Westvleteren as a gift. They have been using it in the novitiate ever since. Everything begins with this sitting. The book's title is not a lie. Törnqvist calls her children's story about the little girl on a pole: *Short Tale about Love* [*Klein verhaal over liefde*].

strangely familiar

Contagious the full
belly-laugh of light.
Without even pricking up your ears
there suddenly it is,
not from afar
nor from nearby,
just slipping round the corners of your lips
impossible to suppress
you could not live with less
and anyway, why would you?

Hans Andreus

There is something paradoxical about desire. That struck me again when I read the book *Tuesdays with Morrie* by Mitch Albom. It's about the author's conversations with a man in the last year of his life, a professor who exerted a major influence on the author during his student years. Years later the professor appeared on a television program. He was suffering from a terminal illness. His days were numbered. Surfing the channels, Mitch catches this and decides to go and look him up. Just like before, they click and they agree that Mitch will visit every Tuesday.

During one of these conversations Morrie, very ill, says how touched he is by the flowers on the windowsill and the breeze that flutters through the open window. He is paralyzed from head to toe and unable to get out of bed. Mitch asks him what he would do if for twenty four hours he could function normally again. He is amazed when Morrie ticks off very ordinary things, like walking in the park, organizing a little dinner with friends. I'm not amazed. I recognize readily what motivated Morrie. When you experience the fragility of life, everyday things acquire an incredible glow. You understand how the ordinary is extraordinary. Everything becomes a source of wonder. It becomes precious, perhaps because you may be about to lose it, and you become aware just how unique and valuable it is.

Life is so strange. Nothing can be more paradoxical. People in the full bloom of life often wrestle with the dullness of their existence. In order to experience some sense of delight they keep looking farther and farther: voyages to distant places, spectacular challenges, etc. While people who feel the power ebbing out of their body sometimes rediscover, unexpectedly, right through the night and the pain, life in all its enchantment. Eye to eye with mortality, they perceive the deep, inexpressible glow that permeates everything . . . the simplest things: the wind softly playing in the window, a flower motionless on the windowsill. Life—death. So hard, so beautiful.

What is longing? Why does it flourish? Why does it wither? I don't know. I don't get it at all. Sometimes I feel it. At other times, absolutely not. We cannot create longing, I think. We can prepare the soil. Nothing more. Hoping that one day it will germinate. Perhaps. I am not talking here about the desires of youth. That is blossoming. That is the drive, the spontaneous joy of living that wells up inside of us when life is going fine and we have the wind at our back. What I mean is the strange, inexpressible longing that can set us afire when all blossoms have blown away. Longing that we experience as a completely unexpected fruit that we no longer thought possible. Longing that has to do with waiting, with having faith, with persevering, and with patiently allowing ourselves to be dug out by life itself.

These days, psychologists and philosophers are always talking about the person as a striving being. In their way of thinking, our sense of life is not dominated by plenitude but by emptiness, shortfall. They describe the human experience in terms of standing in the middle of emptiness, always on a journey. It's a life of striving, of longing, while realizing that there is no end to it. As in a song by Stef Bos: "I am always under way. I live, restless and unsure, between love and emptiness." It's a vision that has its roots in psychoanalysis and that has always attracted me, and still does. Even so, for a good stretch of time I was convinced that all longing had definitely died in me.

What do you have to look forward to when you are told that your days are numbered and that you will be completely incapacitated? In just one stroke, everything lost its glow. I fell into a gigantic depression and could not detect even a glimmer of light. In fact, I was already dead, even before I died. Then something strange happened that I still can't comprehend. Something in me, something I am unable to name, wanted to go deep into stillness, even as I failed to understand why. I remember that very well. I stood looking through the window of my small student room in Leuven, and all of a sudden it rose up in me. It was an impulse and I followed it, even though it went totally against my routine and against everything that until then had been familiar to me. Everybody said I was crazy, but nobody could stop me. This was the time that I was visiting the abbey of Westvleteren and there I met Karin Lelyveld of the Saint Lioba convent in Egmond-Binnen. I saw my opportunity, and I blurted out my strange request. She assented. Two months later I took off, entering the silence of a convent of Benedictine sisters.

I would be lying if I said it was easy. Now I look back on it with gratitude. Then, however, it was a very difficult and particularly painful step to take. It was awful. I was one knot of misery and doubt, and in the first few months I was there the misery and doubt only increased. Everything that I had lost and was about to lose cut into me, razor-sharp. What had I started? Were my parents and friends not right in thinking that this was a ludicrous undertaking? But I am stubborn by nature. I attended the Divine Office with the sisters and spent the time in-between struggling in the silence of my room, even if I could only just hold on. Once in a while I had a conversation with Karin.

Even today I remember how every conversation began. I recollect it clearly because I was shocked each time. "What do you long for?" she asked whenever I sat with her. I was baffled. Where did this come from? How did she dare? As if you have something left to desire when everything is being taken from you! But the repetition of the question, together with the wrestling with myself alone in silence, led me to a longing that I did not know existed. There is much in a human being that can be broken. Just about everything can be damaged: your health, your self-image, your relationships, your dreams. But there is something that cannot be broken. Somewhere deep inside lies something that cannot be violated, by anyone. I find "longing" a nice word to describe it, and in the end it is impossible to express what the longing is for. It is longing, period. It is indefinable. It is open, to everything and everybody. Not that I always understand what is going on. It lies beyond all knowing, grasping, and striving. Sometimes it's there, mostly not. Then there's nothing to do but wait and wrestle. But the discovery of this longing continues to exert an effect on me, even now.

There is a verse in the Old Testament that I have internalized for years. A simple sentence from Hosea: "I am going to seduce her and lead her into the desert, and speak to her heart." Whoever this "I" may be remains unnamable, the mystery of life and death. But to me it's a beautiful phrase. It expresses something of the painful experience that life can be, like being pushed into some kind of desert—but it is precisely there that you are spoken to, deep in your heart.

Even if you can't explain what is happening. It's not a little voice that pops up all of a sudden. But something is being birthed. Something opens up that could not have unfolded if you had not been pushed into the wilderness.

For me, it's exactly there, in that inhospitable place, that a whole new dimension of life has opened up, and I can only wish that everybody may discover it someday. It is a life-giving "layer," deeper than everything, wider and bigger than anything we can imagine. It lies at the very source of our existence. Nonsense remains nonsense, wilderness remains wilderness, but it goes deeper than that. Rather than excluding nonsense, it includes it.

An ex-prisoner expressed this beautifully (once in a while I participate in jailhouse discussion groups). The guy came to talk to all the volunteers involved in the project. He talked about his life before and after prison. It was a tale of unremitting misery. At one point he said, "There is a kind of fish that lives on the ocean floor that has no eyes. These fish are ugly, without eyes. They are banished to a total darkness and a total silence." And then he said something that really struck me: "They survive because of the undying light of hope." That man, just like me, must be passing through a tunnel his whole life long. Where eyes no longer serve and where there are no points of orientation. Darkness everywhere. There is nothing from the outside that can help you anymore. The only thing you have left is the longing of your own heart.

jump into not-knowing

If you understand too much,
eternity passes you by.

Rilke

Laid low by influenza, I am bent over a photobook that attempts to explain to an ordinary layperson like myself modern-day insights into the universe. I feel like I am getting dizzy, and clearly not just because of the flu! Immersing yourself in topics like these, any need to build up an ego disappears. Your jaw literally drops in amazement. A book like that hits you with the painful but also liberating realization of your insignificance and not-knowing. To use an image from Lucebert, our planet is "not more than a breadcrumb on the skirt of the universe." And the whole universe was created out of a pinhead as large as a breadcrumb. Unimaginable! Funny how books like this take me to the same point as the writings of the mystics: confronting the deepest reality, whether that of your own heart or that of the universe, you can only feel dizzy.

For years I had no notion that life actually is something of a dizzying reality. As if I had lived only in the upper two inches of my body. I approached reality totally from my head. Consequently, life could be understood and organized. As a student I focused on philosophy and psychology. I aimed to situate all things within their context and to build an intellectual framework that, to my sense, did justice to the complexity of human beings and the world. I was proud of my clear but nuanced vision. It does not appeal to me anymore. It's all past perfect tense. Now I can and want to say only: I don't know.

The edifice of ideas that I had meticulously built up and that I believed sturdy was blown to smithereens when I had to face my illness and mortality. It was as if a bomb had detonated. To this day I remember how dead and empty my life felt after that explosion. The icy silence. The horrible feeling of having been mortally wounded. The unbearable realization: "This is not going to end well."

The crazy thing is that after a while I began to experience it as some kind of deliverance. Stronger even: what at first was pure horror proved later to be extremely liberating. The collapse of all my beliefs turned me around completely, more drastically than my illness. To such an extent that I almost dare say: I was fortunate that bomb exploded. Never again do I want to squeeze back into the straightjacket of abstract thought. What initially felt dizzyingly empty and dead turned out later to possess an equally dizzying sparkle. It was as if in that unbearable night of total not understanding a new dawn began to shine. So radiant and brisk that it takes my breath away, albeit in not-knowing.

Of course there is an aspect to all this that even today I find unbearable. I do not want to romanticize. Yet, just like the mystics and that book about the universe, I cannot help but sing about how dizzying not-knowing is. But it's more like stammering. "It is as if language splits apart and breaks at the joints," says Kierkegaard. It is important to grasp this. If not, you arrive at gruesome notions. That illness, or losing a child, etc., could be "a mercy," "a blessing," or whatever. Nonsense! Please let's not force it into the straightjacket of intellectual thought.

If there is one thing that I owe to my illness, it is this: labels, frameworks, metaphors—they all have fallen by the wayside. Abruptly, my opinions about life ceased to be relevant. They failed to engage me. Not a single metaphor seemed apt. I thought that I had lost everything. But, not so. I discovered that later. I only had lost the metaphors, not life. In the painful emptiness of no-metaphors something wonderful happened. Instead of living in a world of labels, access to life itself opened up. The best way I can describe it is as a pushing through all possible ideas *about* reality to reality itself. And that reality is infinitely more beautiful, intense, grand, whimsical, and mysterious than the mental images within which we mostly live it and experience it. It teems with life and vibrates with heavenly music.

I never experienced life as intensely as during the year that should have been my last. Not at first. In the beginning, it was pure despair. And I still suffer that despair at times. But sometimes there is something more in it. Right through my despair there were bursts of pure connection: the scents of a departing rain shower, the whispering of the trees, the deep softness of a kitty's fur, the swaying to and fro of flowers on their stems, the sound of a gurgling creek seeking its way, the wild song of birds . . . When I saw everything as it were for the last time, it appeared as if I saw everything for the first time. I saw all things in their unimaginable—I would even say shocking—beauty. I saw them in their mysterious intangibility. I started to understand the meaning of the words of the Apocalypse: I saw a new heaven and a new earth. Not that it eliminates despair. The riddle of suffering remains as large as life. The same for the experience of suffering, which remains with me day in and day out, and yes, it is bitter. But there have been moments of such profound peace and harmony that I cannot say that this illness is only negative.

There is much debate about the meaning of suffering. I also used to wrack my brains over it. Now, I don't give a hoot. No matter where you turn, there is no answer to this question. It's a path that leads nowhere. On the contrary, my experience is that thinking about it only drives me to bitterness. I want to argue for a different track. I have discovered another possibility. At first sight an absurd enterprise . . . In lieu of fighting against the dark of not-knowing, we have to let ourselves be vanquished by it. I have discovered the art of waiting in darkness. We have to dare to persevere in what appears at first to be only emptiness. There is a world strewn with innumerable wonders that awaits those who have freed themselves from the constraints of reasoning. Keats is absolutely right when he exclaims: "Oh, how much more than a life of thought do I prefer a life of experiences!" It's a way of being devoted to, and trusting in, Life itself, rather than to ideas about life.

Nobody lashes out against the limits of reason as the Russian philosopher Shestov. Ton Lathouwers refers to him frequently, and many fragments from Shestov appear in his book *Knocking Where There Is No Gate* [*Kloppen waar geen poort is*], a bundle of *koans.* I read and reread them. The more I read them the more they speak to me. I feel a connection with the fire in this man's soul. I once read an article about Shestov by Maria Stahlie in *NCR Journal of Commerce* [*NCR Handelsblad*]. Stahlie maintains that Shestov's stormy fight against reason, which he kept fighting well into the final weeks of his life, had as its sole purpose the recovery of the most precious prize for mankind: the right to the living God of the Bible. According to Shestov, reason, with its mechanistic rules, cannot possibly fathom the metaphysical explorations that take place behind the wall. Behind the wall, that's the place to be . . . It is there where the capricious, mysterious, impossible to pin down life holds court, directing ways of thinking in which no empirical fact can counter that everything, literally everything, is possible. Behind the wall there is also the living God of the Bible, and not the god who is trimmed by philosophy into an entity utterly bound by the contours of the laws of logic and morality.

For me the words of Shestov have everything to do with what I tried to put into words above. It is the labels of philosophy and theology that, to the extent that they constrain, kill the living God of the Bible. According to him, you only gain access to God (whoever he or she or it may be) through life itself. Today we barely speak of God anymore. But the diminishing of God continues unabated; it continues whenever life is reduced to an entity that cannot expand beyond the contours of any given ideology. Also, we fail to realize that, in effect, we are strangling reality with all our conceptualizing. We fail to understand that we can only get a sense of its vivacious nature in the dark of not-knowing.

Of course, I don't wish to deny that there is incalculable merit to our intellect. Who would want to pick a quarrel with that? But the fundamental error resides in the fact that the intellect itself ignores the limits of its power and potential. Today everything is subjected to reason. While, as Plotinus said, our intellect is no more than a servant. The intellect has value, beyond a doubt, but a limited one. At the same time, I believe it is equally important, if not of the greatest importance, also to cultivate not-knowing.

In not-knowing the living Reality unfolds. As far as I am concerned, no text renders this more beautifully than the Prajnaparamita Sutra (Hymn to the Wisdom beyond all Wisdom). This hymn is sung during the *sesshins* of the Maha Karuna Ch'an. It is a moving song of praise about what is found beyond all knowing. The text consists of several verses, each of which begin with "Greetings be . . ." It is too long to render here in its entirety. I limit myself to a few lines:

> "Greetings be, Wisdom beyond all Wisdom,
> that knows no bounds, surpassing all thinking.
> Your limbs are unspoiled and free,
> And unspoiled are they who experience you.
> (. . .)
> Greetings be, unfathomable Silence, bound by nothing,
> like the infinity of the universe.
> Everybody who truly so experiences you,
> touches the infinity of the Buddha as well.

(. . .)
Greetings be. Who can really praise you,
You who have no face, no image,
You who completely surpass all language,
You who are carried by nothing at all.
(. . .)
Greetings be. As long as we do not try to hold you,
then indeed we touch you,
and the deepest freedom is achieved.
How marvelous and how awe-inspiring . . ."

It strikes me that this Buddhist text addresses a "You" which remains undefined, even though extensively praised and exulted. In the same way, it strikes me that John of the Cross, in his belief in a personal God, can only utter the words "nada, nada, nada" (nothing, nothing, nothing). It points to the unspeakable that is being discovered, and how language is churned and worked over in an effort to say at least something about it.

and still not-knowing

> *Oh, I don't know,*
> *but exist, be beautiful.*
> *Say: look, a bird*
> *and teach me to see the bird.*
> *Say: life is a loaf of bread*
> *to be bitten into and the apples shine red*
> *from pleasure, and more, and more, say something.*
> *Teach me to cry and when I cry*
> *teach me to say: it's nothing*
>
> Herman de Coninck

When all familiar ways of thinking fell to pieces and led to my discovering a richness, everything changed: my outlook on the world, on life, and also on people. I notice that even with respect to people, not-knowing is becoming more and more important to me. I find that what is most important in people remains beyond our reach. The better you know somebody, the more you discover that the other person escapes you completely. He or she is pure mystery. How strongly this contrasts with the labels we put on individuals, sometimes even after only a few minutes. And that when we have just barely met them! I am drawn ever more strongly to the saying of English mystic Evelyn Underhill: "The best thing we can do for those we love is to help them escape from us."

One of the things about André Louf that impresses me enormously is not-judging. It has to do with not-knowing. Because the moment we know, judgment arrives. Then we say: "this is bad," "this is impossible," "this is the way to do it." But I find it liberating to remain in not-knowing. Whatever somebody's life may be, whatever he or she may have done, we cannot judge. We don't know. This enables a real involvement with others. It connects you with another who really is other. Free from my judgments and preferences, I experience every human being in the first place as another with whom I feel a connection.

My studies trained me to think of people in the context of psychological frameworks. Experimental psychology, psychoanalysis, the systems thinking and contextual approach of Nagy, to name just a few, constitute incredibly useful working instruments. I would be the last one to argue with them—I have derived far too much benefit from them myself. But nevertheless, these kinds of frameworks all start with some kind of labeling.

I remember being shocked at my first experience with this. It occurred in a lab in psychological diagnosis. A group of us students sat in a room behind a glass wall. On the other side a psychologist conducted an intake conversation. We listened in, but the other person did not know: the glass was see through only one way. The purpose was for us to learn to pose meaningful questions, and to try to make a diagnosis on the basis of what we heard. I still remember the moment vividly. Some thirty of us were crammed into that packed room. The conversation had barely started when the labeling began. While all of this happened in an educational context, it offended me how quickly and thoughtlessly we fired the craziest diagnoses at that person, and it still bothers me to this day. Deep inside I felt a swell of rebellion: can we do this, is this right? When I mentioned these concerns to my fellow students afterward, they looked at me strangely.

When I reflect on the experience, I believe that was the moment when all "knowing" started to become shaky for me. Or better, that it brought out the doubt. My own confrontation with illness probably had something to do with it. I was already ill at the time. It was the beginning. I still did not know the true extent of what was going on in my body. But something inside of me sharply felt the relativity of all those labels. I experienced a strong resistance to the ease with which diagnoses were thrown around in the lab, and I realize that it came from a budding and early realization that life, including a person's life, is infinitely more mysterious and nuanced than can be expressed in labels.

Shortly afterward came the blow that brought everything down. It turned out that no treatment existed for what ailed me. It also appeared that, if things continued as they were going, I did not have much longer to live. That was when I decided to go to the St. Lioba convent in Egmond-Binnen. One of the sisters at Lioba drew my attention to the fact that in Greek, "psyche," in addition to soul, also means butterfly. I had told her about my studying psychology and we got into a captivating conversation. "Psychology deals with one aspect of the human soul, the aspect that is ill," she said, "and that is important. But I hope that you'll discover that there is another side as well. Because psychology forgets that, just like a butterfly, the soul cannot be grasped." To this day I am struck how this sister—possibly without realizing it herself—alluded to what was happening within me: all my familiar thought frameworks were falling apart. As if she felt that, with all my so-called "knowing," I had landed in a terrible impasse, and she wanted to give me a hint.

I lived with the sisters for over a year, and I discovered that other side. In the quiet that is typical for their way of living, I have learned to regard the human soul in a totally different manner. I found that our innermost self is as staggering as the universe. Shestov expresses it beautifully:

> The well-known expression "to look into someone's soul" appears, at first sight, to be utterly understandable. But if you look closer, it seems to be so unfathomable

> that you wonder if it has any meaning at all. Just try to immerse yourself in another person's soul. You will see nothing but an expansive, empty black abyss. The only thing that happens to you is that, as reward for your effort, it will make you dizzy. But perhaps it is exactly in that obscure chasm that something can be found beyond the dizziness. We need not so much to discover new methods as to learn to look fearlessly into those depths that appear bottomless to the untrained eye. In the end, that emptiness turns out not to be so devoid of meaning after all. Since early childhood we have been inculcated with the idea that the human mind can only grasp so many things, but this only proves that we have to free ourselves from yet another prejudice.

When you have learned to fathom the depths of your own soul in stillness and without fear, it is impossible to accept the strictures of labels for yourself and others, nor do you want to. You have fathomed the limitless depth of the human soul, and in that sounding grows a sense of its deep, hidden meaning. "Perhaps something, even only a glimpse, is then finally revealed to us of that mysterious 'you,' and then maybe also the 'I' will not be so enigmatic," says Shestov. Maybe then we finally reach that which lies beyond all labels, even if it is as vulnerable and impalpable as a butterfly. Is it not there, in that bottomless depth, where our most profound destination opens up, that for which we are truly destined?

Here we have come upon something radically different from the wares offered up by psychology. For me, this discovery constituted a truly liberating step in the midst of a horrible impasse. For what good do all your labels do you when you confront the big unknown of life and death? Eye to eye with death, what is there to save? What is there to know? Against death, we are powerless. Our hands and brains are unable to grasp anything more. We stand naked. It was a shattering experience for me and yet, to be honest, also liberating: when the labeling is over, something else starts to flourish . . .

My computer sits in a room at the back of our house, with a view of the garden. I sat there writing yesterday when all of a sudden I heard a scraping, squeaking sound. My gaze shifted to the outside, to the garden. The weather was brilliant. Not the slightest breeze in the air, everything bathed in a soft, clear light. I saw nothing. Another squeak. Then I had to laugh. Above the weathered garden fence I saw the curly head of Antje appear and disappear. She was on the swing, and loving it. Antje is five. She regularly stays over at her grandmother's, who lives next door. Delighted, I kept looking at my neighbor's little granddaughter. At the enthusiasm with which she surrendered to the swinging, while her curls danced wildly up and down. She was not contemplating theories or explanations. She was just swinging . . . I watched this little girl move with her whole being. Without thinking of anything at all. Completely at one with her activity. And suddenly I wished for life to be such that we would not grow older than five.

things as things

What we see of things are the things.
Why would we see one as if it were another?
Why would we mistakenly see and hear
when seeing and hearing are seeing and hearing?

The key is to be able to see,
to be able to see without thinking,
to be able to see when one sees,
and not to think when one is seeing
nor to see when one is thinking.

But that (woe to us, with our dressed-up souls!)
that requires in-depth study,
requires schooling in unlearning
and imprisonment in the freedom of a convent
of which poets say that the stars are the eternal sisters
and the flowers a day's repentant sinners
but where in the end the stars are just the stars
and the flowers only flowers,
which is why we call them stars and flowers.

Fernando Pessoa

In the beginning of my illness, when there were no assistive computers and I had no personal assistants, I spent many hours at home without anything to do. I devoured book after book until I reached a point of saturation and even reading ceased to be fun. I was bored stiff in those days. One day

I again sat listlessly staring through the window. Outside I saw a bunch of chattering schoolchildren sauntering home, and far away I heard cars whizzing by in the midday traffic. As always when I was confronted with activity, it hurt. I felt deeply unhappy and frustrated. "Everybody is engaged in an active life, and mine is senseless," I whined inside. All of a sudden, though, something clicked. In the lawn, among the withered leaves under the hedge, I saw a blackbird scratching around and the thought came to me: *The manner in which* you're sitting here in this chair is part of the problem. You can drape yourself in the chair in this apathetic way, totally disinterested. Or you can *see* the things around you and be thankful for it. From where this welled up inside of me, I do not know. But all at once the insight was there.

Later I read in the English mystic Evelyn Underhill that happiness resides precisely in that manner of seeing. It is an intuition that many writers and poets have put into words. In all possible forms and languages. Happiness has to do with perception. With seeing what is, *as* it is. With a love for things as things. Witness the above poem by Pessoa.

The starting point of Underhill's fervent argument is a citation from William Blake: "If the windows of our perception were washed clean, everything would appear to us as it is: infinite. However, we have imprisoned ourselves to such an extent that we only see things through the narrow cracks of our cave."

Our windows are smudged, says Underhill. They are covered by the spider webs of our thoughts, our preconceptions, our cowardice and sloth, and that's why we often don't *see* the world as it is. "Through our windows we don't see the world as it 'intrinsically' is, but only that limited little world that is relevant for our own needs, moods, and preferences." In her view, the material for a life that is more intense, for a wider, keener consciousness and a deeper understanding of our own existence, lies right at our doorstep. But we are separated from it. Save in exceptional moments, we barely realize that it is there. That's how much we are captured by our own moods and thoughts.

So there exists such a thing as *pure* seeing. If that is true, then I suffer perhaps more from an *eye* problem than from a muscle disorder. We are so accustomed to seeing the world through the cracks of our own cave that we take it for granted. Underhill is right: we don't even realize it. It's our spontaneous way of seeing. We naturally see everything through the cracks of what *we* think is important and likeable.

That's how we go through life, sometimes pleased and sometimes disappointed, happy or frustrated, depending on whether or not life responds to our desires. A bad mishap renders us bitter and hopelessly frustrated, as happened with me. The fact of the matter is that reality quite frequently does not meet our expectations. When a misfortune happens, our expectations are not met in any way or shape. The unceasing, bottomless frustration of my life has opened my eyes to the question: How do I *look* at all things? Not as a philosophical question but a practical one. Is there a way of seeing that does not continually lead to frustration? I cannot change my illness. The limits imposed by ALS cannot be undone. But perhaps there are other boundaries that can be moved.

Evelyn Underhill mentions that in exceptional moments, a penetrating realization of a world *beyond* and *alongside* of us can impose itself, and how liberating that is. This rings a bell with me. I still remember clearly how, at the nadir of "falling ill and losing everything," I sat in a church and heard a thrush singing. It was so sonorous that it seemed as if I heard its whistle for the first time in my life. It filled me with an unfamiliar happiness and a tranquil confidence, even though at that moment things really did not look good for me. I am reminded of the true story by a Russian author about a young conscript at the front during World War II. The soldier lies half submerged in a morass, mortally wounded. A friend keeps vigil nearby during his final hours. All of a sudden, the dying soldier says: "That dragonfly, is it still there?" Then he passes away.

Eye to eye with death, a marvelous, liberating consciousness of the things around us can rush in: a thrush, a dragonfly . . . as if the great powers of suffering, death, and mourning work a simplification in us that makes us see things differently. Perhaps making us *really* see for the first time. Underhill makes the point that the forces of beauty, astonishment, and love sometimes can bring about the same effect and that we, in one way or another, all experience such exceptional moments. For me it happened when I found myself at a horrible low point. That's not, however, the way it has to be. It can be different. But no matter how, these moments make us realize that we spend our everyday lives in a closed and stuffy little world. All the while our human inheritance actually consists of a world of morning glory, in which every titmouse is a heavenly ambassador and in which every bud swells with the full meaning of existence.

Does Plato not express the same thing with his well-known allegory of the cave dwellers? That we live in a cave, with the shadows of our thoughts, and we have only the most basic notion of the thrilling, living world outside.

In the introduction to the fourteenth century mystical work *The Cloud of Unknowing*, André Zegveld uses the image of a child running through the hallway to convey to the reader how imprisoned we are by ideas and, as a consequence, the price we pay in a lack of vitality. He writes: "A child experiences the length of the hallway by running and its height by yelling, while we, adults, remain standing at the door, able to express the length only in dry, meaningless meters." I know that the adult, who says that the hallway is twenty-five meters long and three meters high, has more knowledge than the child that runs and screams. But has the adult also not lost something? Haven't we all lost something? Are the words of Huub Oosterhuis not applicable to each one of us? "Reawaken my softness. Give me back the eyes of a child. So that I see what is, and trust, and don't hate the light."

I started reflecting on these kinds of insights, in confrontation with myself, my illness, and later, the words of Underhill. I became aware that we have indeed lost something fundamental. What exactly? I would say: the intensity and the simplicity with which we as children could observe a beetle in the grass. Our vision has become cloudy instead of uninhibited and unselfconscious. Our way of observing has ceased to be pure. That was a fundamental discovery for me, which I encounter again and again. It is, apparently, universal. Our way of knowing is mediated by our thoughts, theories, feelings, habits, and needs. In itself, that's not bad. It is, actually, necessary for organizing our life. But as a result, we have lost our direct connection with every thing, our spontaneous experience of reality. What abundance, what freedom, what delight awaits us if we, with our dressed-up souls, would only dare to offer ourselves up to the school of unlearning that so enriches Pessoa . . .

In reading all this, the question may arise: All well and good, but how do you do it? How can we cut loose from our thoughts, feelings, and habits? How can we regain the capacity to experience directly? In rare moments, it happens spontaneously. But how about more generally?

One thing is sure. It is not easy. Underhill does not mince words: "My answer is that you can achieve this through a course of training, the first phases of which will be tough to bear." With some irony, she adds: "If it doesn't require the self-abnegation of the convent, then at least the discipline of the golf course." Algerian Sufi master Bentounès says similarly: "If a way is not demanding when starting upon it, beware." So, the path to union with reality follows a route of arduous training. We will have to cultivate another way of seeing. We will need to succeed in simplifying and disciplining our outlook and our heart. This is only possible if we suspend our needs, moods, and preferences. In other words, this is going to require work—on ourselves!

Underhill counsels her readers to practice *mindfulness* and *unselfishness*, "even if in the beginning it may feel a lot like war." According to her, we can regain that simplicity of outlook and heart if we maintain the practice. *How* it happens, nobody knows. It's not a technique. It's not because you practice that you automatically get a hold of that other way of seeing. It's like bicycling. You try, fall, try, fall, until suddenly you realize with surprise: I am riding. How you did it, nobody knows. All of a sudden, you got it. Or rather, it got you. You can also compare it with sleeping: you can undress, put on your pajamas, lie down, switch off the light, remain quiet, empty your head. But even so, you can only wait for sleep to come. The emptying and quieting in Zen meditation is, for me, such a practice in unlearning. It's a strange exercise in mindfulness and unselfishness, bicycling and sleeping.

what confuses

Eternity cannot be understood.
You observe it.

Marguerite Yourcenar

With some people, I always start by talking about books. Flemish cabaret singer Willem Vermandere is one of them. It all began when I heard him sing at a concert in the Netherlands. Hearing your own familiar dialect in another country is delightful, and we easily slipped into a conversation. I was living in the Netherlands at the time, and we kept up the contact. After my return to Belgium, he invited me to come and stay with him at his home in Steenkerke. His wife put a bed in a garden hut that only contained books. For three full days I withdrew into this book-filled hermitage, immersed in the luxuriant green of the garden and a similarly luxuriant world of words.

During that time one of his daughters came every day to sculpt in his atelier. Father and daughter engaged with the stone while I disappeared in the books. We only saw each other in the kitchen during meals or for a cup of coffee. The conversations in that kitchen were of a rare intensity, probably because we came to them out of our solitariness. Being by ourselves for hours on end, with a rock or a book, gave these encounters a special coloring. We reached a different level. As if words penetrated deeper because of the stillness and, as a result, when they surfaced they were possessed of an inside and felt lived in. Over the kitchen table these two artists told me about the writers that mattered to them. Next to a passion for stone, they apparently also had a passion for books. That people exist who hunger after words—people who *lived* by words—was a revelation to me.

When I left, Willem Vermandere advised me to dip into a book every single day. Even if just for a page or a poem. I am still grateful to him for his counsel. I enjoyed books prior to my stay in Steenkerke. But there I learned the value of discipline in reading. Just like the monks' *lectio divina* but with novels, literature, and poetry. Reading daily *and* reading slowly. Patiently absorbing the text. Like cows chew the cud, chewing the words, to use the expressive image used by the monks. "It builds a layer of humus inside of you," the cabaret singer impressed on me. "And one day wondrous things will sprout from that layer of humus. People believe I just make up my songs and stories, but in reality each and every one is the fruit of years of reading." I don't compose songs, I don't invent stories. But I live off the rich harvest from the humus of sustained reading.

When I saw Willem Vermandere again a while ago, it appeared that we were both reading Kertész. Imre Kertész is a Jewish-Hungarian writer. He received the Nobel Prize for literature in 2002. I fell under the spell of his books. Apparently, Willem Vermandere had as well. No book has moved me as much in recent years as *Kaddish for a Child Not Born.* A short work, masterfully written. It's a monologue in which Kertész attempts to put into words why he never wanted to bring a child into the world. A father's elegy for an unborn child that he, in this way, wanted to spare his own fate. A book that hurts, by a person who's kicking and screaming from the pain of smearing his life onto the pages, with subtlety but mordantly.

As a young boy in 1944, Imre Kertész was picked up and deported to Auschwitz. After the war he returned to Budapest. He used his experiences to write his best-known work, *Fatelessness* [*Onbepaald door het lot*]. This autobiographical novel forcefully describes the experiences of a fifteen-year-old in the concentration camps of Auschwitz, Buchenwald, and Zeitz. Imre Kertész did not choose the subject matter of his oeuvre. All his books deal with the holocaust. That in itself moves me, because I recognize it. Even though I'm not a novelist, I know the bitter experience of devastating injury. The urge to come face to face with it by writing, a whole life long, even if it never succeeds. As Kertész says somewhere, "Writing in the hope someday to get to know your hope." To have no other choice. Unable to do otherwise. To have to, willing or not.

Kaddish for a Child Not Born is thoroughly affecting. Kertész's story is dark and cynical, pages on end. Yet it is not just a book of despair. In the darkest night, suddenly a shimmer shines through, a light so rare, so pure, it's breathtaking.

At one point Kertész recounts the experience that marked him most at Auschwitz. To my surprise, it is not death but life. Young Kertész was being transported. Critically ill, he lay on a stretcher on the platform of a train station. He had not yet received his ration. It was actually placed next to another emaciated prisoner, a man called "the Professor." Then, for no apparent reason, Kertész is lifted up and moved close to the next wagon. And all of a sudden he sees how "the Professor" runs toward him, shoves him his food ration, hisses "Well, what did you expect . . . ?" and returns to his place, having put his own life at immediate peril. The experience that somebody could be indignant because he, Kertész, no longer wanted or had the courage to live, that somebody would risk his own life for that, as if that life also were not something holy, that spontaneous reaction, that impulse of choosing life, caused more consternation to Kertész than the thousand faces of death that surrounded him daily.

He writes: "There *is* something—and, again, I beg you, don't try to label it—there exists a pristine concept untainted by all strange material circumstances: our bodies, our souls, the raging wild beasts in our bosoms; an idea that exists in the minds of all of us as an identical concept, yes, an idea whose preservation, protection, constituted his, 'the Professor's,' *only genuine chance* for survival. The chance for survival without adherence to this idea was for him no chance at all, because without the preservation, the pristine, undisturbed valuation of this concept, he did not *wish* to, or what's more, probably *could* not live."

That last sentence says it all for me. Extracted from the rawest reality. *Lectio divina* at its best, if you ask me. A sentence that penetrates to the core. Again and again, throughout the ages, there is this discovery, even in the darkest night: there *has* to be something . . . and the most poignant part of it is that Kertész asks to leave this perfectly pure something unnamed.

The hell that is the holocaust is, according to Kertész, not incomprehensible but, on the contrary, easy to understand. Evil is predictable. We can analyze it perfectly, explain it in detail. What causes confusion is the good. Goodness is unintelligible, because there is no rational explanation for it. He writes: "For that very reason I am no longer interested in Führers, Chancellors, or other sundry titled usurpers, regardless of how many interesting details you muster concerning their spiritual worlds; no, instead of the lives of dictators, it is, exclusively and for a long time now, the lives of the saints that interest me. This is what I find interesting and incomprehensible, this is what I cannot find a rational explanation for."

At some level, it is shocking to read this. If you think of all the misery suffered in the camps, the incomprehensibility of evil assaults you like a devastating tsunami. Kertész turns things upside down. But looking at it closer, I can't say he's wrong. His words are evidently true. The evil in my life is also totally explainable. The wild beasts that rage within me, I know them and understand them, each and every one. I know where they come from and when they run wild. Explosions of anger, fits of jealousy and bitterness, bouts of callousness and irritability, these are all eminently understandable in the context of my life. Also, the evil that I suffer is predictable and easy to understand: when people avoid me, belittle me, patronize me, show fear or disgust. The same with evil in the world. It's not difficult to explain.

Confusing and surprising, totally unintelligible, and impossible to eradicate is the urge in me to remain a human being, notwithstanding the dehumanizing nature of my illness and my environment. Beyond understanding is the attitude of my husband who, against all logic, enjoys being with me; who shares this difficult life with me, even though in a certain way it will ultimately only result in loss. Beyond understanding is the goodness, completely altruistic, that surfaces in the world, everywhere, over and over again.

This reminds me of a moving television report about the son of a Jewish woman who was killed in a Palestinian bomb attack. Right after the attack, she was asked if her son's heart could be used to save a Palestinian child. She consented. With much pain, but she did. The Palestinian woman offered her gratitude and asked for a photo of the young man so she could hang it in her child's room. You witnessed the conversation between the two women, the sensitivity with which they respected each other's grief, their courage.

In one of his *teishos*, Zen teacher Frank de Waele talked about Mother Teresa. He was in the process of reading her letters. It appears that her whole life the saint from Calcutta wrestled with doubt, despair, and a feeling of having been abandoned by God. Her inner life was one long, dark night. Even so, all these years she remained faithful to implementing her profound desire: to pick the neglected up from the streets.

Incomprehensible goodness. Doing what is simply right, against the current of dehumanization. So there has to be something . . . fascinating. Totally surprising. Confusing.

my desert

Nobody knows himself
who has not suffered.

Alfred de Musset

René Voillaume points out the value of the desert, even if it has no value to the world in and of itself. "Compared with the smaller, fertile, and therefore also overpopulated, areas of our planet, deserts occupy a huge surface. They serve no good purpose, are a thorn in our side and a source of aggravation. They are as meaningless and offensive as the pure adoration, of which they are the outward manifestation. The desert shows us our fundamental powerlessness, and leaves us no choice but to look for strength in God."

Fascinating words, to my mind. The paradox that the desert is at the same time a place of total uselessness and a place for pure adoration (whatever that may be). In any event, a place of extremes. The paradox is that we discover something priceless in something that is vexing and worthless. It is also the paradox expressed by Hisamatsu in the *koan*: "Go stand where there is no place to stand." Carla Pols expresses the same paradox when she says: "Maybe you have already come so far that you no longer know where to look. Then It comes on its own." But I am not that far yet!

This reminds me of a conversation I had with a friend. How he dreams of going off by himself into some desert. At which I promptly threw at him: "A person is ready to go to any kind of desert. He's willing to sit anywhere. As long as it's not in his own desert."

A long silence hung between us. Apparently my words had hit him hard. I myself had to swallow a couple of times. The words had escaped me before I properly understood what they meant. They turned immediately on me. They also burst my illusions. I also hanker after deserts . . . in far-away abbeys, in desolate areas and inhospitable natural environments, in the night's darkness, in *sesshins*, in the big cities. Only my physician was able to keep me from going to live for a month with the Touaregs in the desert of Niger. But don't talk to me about the desert that rages in my own body and that is ruining any kind of "human" life!

I flee from that desert. I shrink from its relentless hardship. I shun it like death. I cannot look at its bone-chilling countenance of barrenness. The mirror that it holds up to me fills me with fear. It shows me things I'd rather not see. I experience it as a horrible, lonely no-man's-land. No thank you. The desert of my body is for me and the world around me a thorn in the flesh. An indignation. As senseless as it is offensive. It deprives my life of purpose, reduces it to something of no significance, of zero value. It renders me a miserable wretch. It's all well and good for me to say that deserts fascinate me. But as long as I want to ignore that desert, the words sound hollow.

Even so, that is the only desert that is real for me. It is *my* desert. If I want to go and sit in a desert somewhere, this is the desert that I must dare to enter. Fingers crossed . . .

I find no roads there. And no water. It's where I die death after death.

If I don't look for strength in God, I am lost.

ever . . .

Begin to believe,
that a certain life on earth is possible,
an everyday life but with love as heartbeat
and with happiness not only for the man,
the woman and the child,
but in surrender to the other,
every other—
with people as children,
friends, partygoers.
People.

Hans Andreus

Tired after a day of wandering about the Inishowen peninsula in Donegal, we end up where we started: in the hamlet Culdaff. We are about to enter our lodgings, but I am held back by a noise. I take a step backward. Apparently, the house next to our B & B is an Irish pub. But a pub, really? It did not at all resemble the pubs we saw on the tourist routes in Ireland. It looked more like an old-fashioned common village alehouse. From time to time the door swung open and a macho type came barreling out. "We're not going to go in there," said my travel companion. The music reverberated and subsided in the street according to the door's opening and closing. Well, yes.

We swing through the door, our turn. Inside, we don't know what we are seeing. The music has stopped. In a corner of the smoky room a small podium is erected where the musicians were just offered a serious pint of Guinness. That should keep them happy for a while, I think. We sit down and also order a pint. Provided with drink and a chair, I look around. The hotchpotch of people is impossibly strange. It looks like a cross section of the village. An old man closes the bathroom door behind him and shuffles to his chair. A twentysomething occupies a barstool. Bent over, head on the counter, he's sleeping it off. A few macho guys his age run busily back and forth, tapping him on the back in passing. Two middle-aged women in short skirts pull themselves onto barstools as well, after having made a jaunty entrance, in their high heels, to the accompaniment of the necessary whistles. At the same time, a boy of fourteen appears out of nowhere. No idea where he comes from. A woman of some age, presumably the owner, serves everybody with drink and her strong perfume. There is a lot of talk, but we don't understand a thing. Some people are simply sitting, like the man next to us. He is not young and appears lonely. All of these people exude loneliness in their own way. They seem marked, no matter the cause: boredom, age, isolation, sadness, unrequited desire, unanswered love.

Suddenly the three musicians pick up their instruments: a guitar, a small flute, and some sort of percussion instrument. They throw themselves into a typical Irish rhythm and start a song. They play and sing with abandon. Again, we don't understand a word. But you see and feel that these people are singing their heart out, their desire, their hope. All at once I felt like an intruder. We were the only tourists. A certain shyness came over me. This was their life, their village, their nostalgia, their pain, and we were its silent witnesses. It felt almost like something intimate, this strange, folksy happening that you don't see anymore where we live. Terrible, and at the same time terribly beautiful. Rarely have people touched me as deeply as there in Culdaff, that hamlet of no significance.

It's a month and half later and I sit in a crammed hall. It's suffocatingly hot and folks are pushing to secure a seat. This is an orientation meeting for parish workers engaged in pastoral care. Would I want to say a word about my relationship to the Bible? I had accepted the invitation with hesitation. Evenings of this sort are totally not my thing. And yet, when I spoke, I saw all these people sitting in front of me. I said something about Job. That his despair brought him closer to God and his fellow men than the assuredness of his friends. That you don't control what happens to you. But that the art of the deal is to bear both your happiness *and* your sorrow in such a manner that it does not isolate you from your neighbor. I noticed the attention with which people were listening. I saw in their faces that they had a lot going on inside. *What* it did to them I could not discern. Only *that* something affected them. And again, a certain shyness fell over me. Again, there was that strange feeling of being moved . . . by each one of them.

I sometimes also notice it when I am just among people, even in the strangest places: the train station, a party, a concert hall. I can be seized by a kind of aloneness, some sort of separation, something of a deep quiet . . . and in that state it happens: a losing of oneself in the other, a strange feeling of being touched by all these people. I look at them, or rather, they look at me with something that I cannot grasp or name. And then there is that poignant emotion, a kind of embrace. It doesn't always happen. Most of the time it does not. Often I rather experience a feeling of estrangement as I mingle among people. But sometimes it catches me: people as children, friends, partygoers. People.

It is the experience, as Indian Zen teacher AMA Samy once expressed it at a reading, of being a human being among human beings. AMA Samy has a double background. He lives in two traditions. He is a Jesuit as well as a Zen teacher. Somebody asked him: "Are you a Buddhist or a Christian?" He burst out laughing, and roared: "But I am a human being!"

That experience, that you are, beyond everything that separates us, underneath all the differences, a human being among human beings.

For me, moments like that touch on the "borderless solidarity" experienced by Christian monks when, immersed in quietude, they descend into the reality of their own heart. These are moments in which you discover that you are "connected" with everybody, without exception. Including the person who spontaneously evokes only abhorrence and antipathy. It is also the deep solidarity tasted in the silence of *zazen*. The Dharani sutra of the Great Compassionate One deals with "entering into the heart that listens." I get emotional each time I hear that sutra sung. "That I may enter into this heart that listens. It is the fullness of all meaning, the ground and purification of all that lives."

That is the way I experience it also. Those who descend into their own heart discover in its depths this listening heart that is the "ground" of all that lives. And the discovery of this heart that listens, of this unlimited solidarity at the bottom of our own heart, is actually nothing else than the realization of our elemental poverty and vulnerability. The experience that, fundamentally, we all confront life "naked and destitute" *and* "blessed" at the same time. Every single one of us, without distinction. As far as I am concerned, nowhere is this realization expressed as beautifully and as lively as in the Prajnaparamita sutra of Rahulabhadra (The Hymn to the Wisdom beyond all Wisdom). The listening heart, the ground of all that lives, receives in that hymn the name of "You." And this You signifies: "blessing" shared by everyone, without exception. But nobody can hold on to it. Nobody can appropriate that blessing. The text says: "Greetings be, the person who sees You is still in bounds. But so is the person who does not see You. And it is also true that the one who sees You is freed, even as the person who does not see You." These words express for me something of the unintelligibility and intangibility of the sense of solidarity that briefly lights up when, while I am among people, a stillness assails me, a strange emotional stirring.

The next person to speak at this orientation evening was the artist-calligrapher Jan Rossey. His creations were shown in a PowerPoint presentation on a large screen. He commented on each one. The impressive thing was that it went from an enormous tangle to complete simplicity. First appeared complicated compositions, succeeded by playful wisps. Poems, fragments of texts, citations, stories, from whatever was close to his heart. There was a swarm of letters against a background of sculpted art. Gradually the compositions became more sober, until, here and there, they simply expressed a sentence in the midst of empty space. At the end his calligraphy became limited to the expression of a single word. "I aim for a sort of minimalism," he said. "I have searched for a long time how to summarize hope in as few words as possible. I arrived at the beautiful word 'ever. . .' For me, it summarizes the whole Bible."

I cannot shake the calligraphic image of "ever . . ." It reminds me of the power of haikus. Trifles. Short little sentences. But they express so much. Just like these few brushstrokes by Jan Rossey. Never have I seen a more accurate expression of hope! Also, for me, this single word "ever" touches on that indefinable poignancy that I sometimes see in people's faces. It shines a light on another facet of the limitless solidarity that is experienced in stillness. Eyes that convey, somehow, an ineradicable hope, an ineradicable longing, no matter what, even in brokenness. Ever . . .

going against gravity

Bind a word on my heart.
Shoe my feet with names.
Lay a path upon the waves.

Huub Oosterhuis

Truly, silence is for me also a way of operating. I think of a phrase by Huub Oosterhuis that challenges me in this area. I read it years ago on a calendar in our bathroom. “Try to live differently with your sorrow: so that it no longer embitters and isolates; and live with your good fortune and well-being so that you don’t become arrogant and unapproachable to the unfortunate.” That morning I returned to the breakfast table with a sigh. My life and indeed the world would look vastly different if people lived that way. To which my husband replied: “In this world, Oosterhuis’s words are not reality. And as long as we live, they never will be. What matters is the vision. His words point to the direction that we must move toward.”

Is that right? Do I really have to accept that sorrow embitters and isolates? That those who have received abundantly are often unapproachable to those with less good fortune? It’s true, you see it happen around you all the time and I catch it in myself: the tendency to see only your own hurt when you’re not comfortable in your skin and, on the other side, when you’re happy, the inclination to be totally caught up in it, blind to those less lucky. I don’t think we do this consciously, out ‹f egoism. It's much more innocent. Something unconscious makes us act that way, and because of that it is very difficult to break through. It is egocentrism. As if it were a spontaneous, natural reflex: me first, then the others . . .

It's as if some kind of law of gravity operates in the way we deal with the world. An iron logic through which things, without the action of a countervailing force, always flow in the same direction: that of self-preservation. It is a reflex that is so very human, even necessary. We can't do without it. But it has a horrible other side: without a countervailing force, we are blind to others. This is less noticeable in people who are lucky than in those who are less fortunate, but in both cases the same law operates: a seeking or a complaining that, in the first instance, disregards the person next to us.

All human interaction seems to occur within the chalk lines of a few subtle mechanisms. I call them subtle because they carry you along almost imperceptibly. If you don't offer resistance, these mechanisms will control you, guaranteed. Your life runs within these preestablished bounds without your realizing the distress you are causing. Here is another one of these subtle mechanisms—I wanted to write a thesis about it (and I would have done it if my illness had not interfered): our tendency to claim credit for successes and to shove the blame for mishaps on forces beyond ourselves (circumstances, education, others, rotten luck).

I think of the saying: "Success has many fathers, but misfortune is an orphan." Another one of these subtle mechanisms. Everyone shows up immediately to garner the laurels of success or to participate in its celebration. But for the one who faced adversity and failure, he knows—if he's honest—that he's had a hard time with it. We don't like to deal with those who are poor and those who failed in life. We like it even less if we are the ones who are poor or marked by failure. We prefer to wrap ourselves in the psychological comfort of "being somebody." Something in us causes us to prefer keeping a safe distance from those who are damaged. We prefer to run a wide circle around misfortune. At least I do.

I try not to blame anybody for this. Sometimes that's hard, because I suffer when these mechanisms operate in others. Anybody who fights poverty, in one way or another, has suffered as a result. But I know all too well that I myself am not free of them. Further, I realize that most people, just like me, do not mean harm. Who does not agree that every person on earth deserves happiness? But in order to achieve even a smidgen of that, the fact is that we have to work against our own spontaneous reactions. The problem is that our thinking and our acting are driven by different motivating forces. It is not because there is right thinking that there is also right action. If we don't engage with ourselves, if we don't offer resistance to our natural tendencies, if we don't become conscious of ourselves, we remain conditioned in all we do by the urge for happiness and self-preservation, and even more so by the fear of misfortune, no matter how exalted our thoughts may be.

Religion offers a countervailing force to the extent that it challenges us to see the face of the other while at the same time showing us our own true face. All great traditions show us ways to grow into real human beings by going against that force of gravity. The phrase by Oosterhuis on the calendar in our bathroom challenges me personally in the hardest way. You don't control fortune or misfortune. It happens to you. But the art lies in learning to receive happiness or to bear sorrow in such a way that you are still mindful of the other.

In my life, marked by the misfortune of an incurable disease, it means this: not to allow myself to drown in waves of sadness. Once in a while, alright, but then I have to resume the battle with these dark waters. The words of Oosterhuis demand, in my case, that I erect dikes against the pain so that pieces of land appear that allow those around me to stand and to live. It is so tempting to let yourself be driven by bitter complaining, to hide completely behind your sorrow, and to slap another around the ears with a "how dare you?" if he or she puts your sorrow in perspective. Is it not equally seductive to allow yourself to glow in the warmth of your good fortune and success, pushing well to the side any questioning or any attempt to put it in perspective (because of the misfortune of a person next to you), so that your precious happiness is not disturbed?

My husband's remark that morning, that the words of Oosterhuis are not of this world, worked as a mirror. It made me realize that I myself am not free of the force of gravity. This is what I attempt, little by little: not to push away the darkness within me, not to identify with my good intentions, but to face straight on that iron law within myself. By falling and getting up I learn "to fly against the force of gravity," as my husband put it during our breakfast conversation. We cannot but accept the force of gravity. It's the nature of the beast. We are all subject to it. Without the urge to self-preservation we cannot survive. But the purpose cannot be that we live as worms pressed flat against the ground. We are made to fly. What matters is to accept the gravitational pull and to use it in such a way that flying becomes possible. Only if I accept that sorrow naturally overflows am I able to build dikes against it. As long as I resist that dark water I deny its existence within me or I see only my good intentions, and then there is not much room left for the person next to me. The words of Oosterhuis are a *verb* that can only be conjugated in the first person.

tsimtsum

We did not inherit
the earth from our forebears,
we only borrowed it
from our children.

Native American wisdom saying

This sentence of Native American origin is displayed above the exit door of the A. S. Adventure store in our neighborhood. Every time I pass the cash register, I feel these words staring at me. My thoughts catch. With our way of life, how far removed are we from this wisdom? Do we behave as people who received the earth only on loan? Or, rather, are we not consuming the earth as if it were our supper?

Along these same lines, I recently read in the paper a news item that shocked me: "September 25, 2009, is Overshoot Day." The article continued: "The earth increasingly fails to keep up with the speed of human consumption. Our urge to consume makes that today, September 25, we have already used up all raw materials that the earth can produce in one year. At this moment, demand surpasses supply by 40%. Thus we live as if we disposed of 1.4 planets." It appears that Overshoot Day comes earlier every year. The first Overshoot Day was December 31, 1986. Ten years later, people already used 15 percent more than the earth could deliver. At that time Overshoot Day fell in November. This year, just over twenty years after the first time, Overshoot Day moved up to September 25.

Every time I recite the First Vow of the Bodhisattva, the earth issue flashes through my mind. "No matter how numerous the living beings may be, I commit to liberate them all." But will there be an earth left for the living beings after we are gone? For me this question is gradually starting to resemble a *koan*. The Jewish-French philosopher Levinas says that an appeal is being lodged by "the face of the other." When I met him at his home in Paris, in the context of a seminar on his philosophy, he said that this face of the other also refers to future generations. Hence, we must take care of the environment. These words made an impression on me. They are a call to action. Today more than ever.

I never realized this more clearly than during a five-day retreat with Benoît Standaert, a Benedictine from Bruges. We spent the days considering his book *Spirituality or the Art of Living* [*Spiritualiteit als levenskunst*], in which he offers an alphabet of monastic practices. These are practices that work transformations, and they have to do with the art of living. They have been tested for years within the walls of abbeys but are certainly equally applicable outside. With the force of lived experience, the monk succeeded in warming us to the tradition in which he lives, and in surprising ways he linked it to the stories, proverbs, and practices of other traditions. Everything can become an exercise in the art of living, including confrontation with the questions of our time, and even ordinary, daily things like eating and drinking.

One morning, Benoît Standaert dropped the word *tsimtsum*. I had never heard it before. The word is derived from the Hebrew verb *tsum*. In the Kabbalah it is used to denote God's act of creation. In the beginning, before God had created anything, only God existed. He occupied everything, from beginning to end. How then could God create something outside himself? Jews say: by shrinking himself. God did tsimtsum. He fasted on himself. He shrunk himself, "as the sea withdraws and makes the continent appear." Rabbi Jehuda Loew warns: "God does everything in order not to be everything. This allows the human being to appear on the scene with his freedom. But if, on his part, the human being fails to do the same thing, then he will fill all that emptiness. Even worse: he becomes everything, in a totalitarian way."

"Culturally, what are we doing today?" Benoît Standaert tossed to us that morning. "Are we not plundering the biosphere, gorging on it, devouring it, notwithstanding all the agreements made in Kyoto?"

With a blazing rage that bordered on the prophetic, he pointed to the danger of a culture that never fasts. In his view, a person who never fasts lives in a fullness that sooner or later chases everybody else away, steamrolling over everybody, reducing everything to himself, until only one world remains, his, until there is nothing different left, or simply until there is nothing left at all. I was shocked by the vehemence of this otherwise so mild and gentle monk. As if he were lit by a holy fury.

Fasting is really not my thing. For me it's a word that reeks of stale air. But this Jewish tsimtsum moved me. Fasting in order to create a space for something other than yourself. Fasting to rein yourself in because of the other. Fasting as an assumption of responsibility. It makes me think of vegetarianism in Buddhism. A form of fasting that has the same kind of meaning, it seems to me. To limit yourself out of respect for other sentient beings. I cannot help but think of our culture's obsession with eating. It looks like we all suffer under the dictatorship of the waist. We would give anything to have an ideal figure. We diet and exercise till we drop. Isn't this also some kind of fasting? And doesn't it also smell a bit? When we fast, at most we create an emptiness in our stomach. But we remain full of ourselves. We are occupied with *our* health, *our* slender figure. How different this Jewish tsimtsum! Instead of being focused on ourselves, it is focused on the world. To fast in that sense is a political, and indeed a cosmic, act. An act of wisdom, balance, respect, responsibility. People who practice tsimtsum are ready to limit themselves, to rein themselves in, so that there will be a world left for the next generation. If you take the newspaper item about Overshoot Day seriously, does fasting not become a duty? And it goes without saying that it's not just about eating.

Sometimes I think that culturally, we are under the spell of an insatiable hunger because we are no longer able to engage with death. In this connection, the novel *Night Train to Lisbon* struck a chord with me. The book is a masterful allegory of modern life: the person who sees all support systems vanish in the mist . . . belief in God, belief in the other person, belief in oneself. The honesty with which Amadeu, the principal character, analyzes himself and his environment is admirable and touching. But then the novel takes a peculiar turn.

Past fifty, Amadeu falls passionately in love with Estefânia, who is twenty-eight years younger. Together with his friend Jorge, they are active in the underground resistance. Estefânia is Jorge's girlfriend. When Jorge wants to kill her because word of the resistance has leaked out and Estefânia knows too much, Amadeu intervenes. He flees the country with the young woman. Along the way a passionate relationship develops. Amadeu wants to start a new life with her in some other place but, even though she has fallen in love with him, Estefânia refuses. She does so with the remarkable words: "You are too hungry for me. I cannot do it. I cannot." Years later, she says:

> He asked me to stop and he embraced me. After that, he kept asking me, more frequently. The avalanche broke. He was searching for me. But it was just that: he wasn't searching for *me*, he was searching for *life*. He wanted more of it, and he always wanted it faster and greedier. . . . Even though now it sounds as if Amadeu was really passionately interested in *me*, it wasn't so. For it wasn't an *encounter*. He sucked with everything he knew, mainly *material of life* he couldn't get enough of. To put it another way, I wasn't really *somebody* for

> him, but rather a *scene* of life he reached for as if he had previously been cheated of it. As if he wanted to live a whole life once more before death overtook him.

Live life like a glutton before the Grim Reaper gets to you appears to be many people's motto. And yet, it is possible to live differently. I feel this very strongly whenever the following sentence is read during *sesshins*: "This I want to impress on all of us: life and death are serious business. All things pass quickly. Hence always be awake, never inattentive, never careless." It's a text that moves me every time, especially when I hear it in the evening, after a day in complete silence. Ton Lathouwers once pointed out that the actual text reads: "Life-death is serious business." The Chinese ideogram for life is the same as for death. The Chinese have only one word to express life and death.

It is an intuition that is found in all spiritual traditions: life and death make up one whole. Jews express this beautifully. They say people should carry two pieces of paper in their pockets. On the first one is written: "Recall, oh you mortal, that you are ash, and to ash you will return." The second says: "On your account the whole world was created."

The Sufis also have a wonderful perspective on life and death. Moslems pray five times a day. Aloud in the morning, because it is still semidark. You don't see too well. You don't know who God is, who you yourself are. You are searching. But at noon Moslems pray in silence. Because the noon prayer is the prayer of adulthood. At noon the sun stands in its zenith, perpendicular in southern countries. It no longer throws off shadows. A person in the noontime of his life, around forty, must begin to understand what matters, say the Sufis. God's light is in full splendor then. At that time you have to achieve maturity. You have to know then what is truly important and assume your responsibility. According to the Sufis, the fact that after noon the sun descends, that we get older and move inexorably toward death, is an invitation to search also in our lifetime for the invisible, for what reaches beyond this life.

As long as you push your death away, and it comes inevitably, you will live more and more greedily. If you look your own mortality in the eye and you entrust yourself to the mystery of life-death, space naturally opens up for everything around you and for everything that will come after you. In any event, that is my experience. When I fell ill and it looked like I would lose everything, my first reaction was a compulsive grasping. I did not want to waste any time. I wanted everything. Here. Now. Immediately. Greedily I tried to squeeze the last ounce out of what was left. But, of course, I lost it anyway, and I arrived at a point where I did not want anything anymore. At the end of my wits, I confronted my possible death. I saw my life as it was and is: transitory and fragile. I risked the jump to something like surrender to the great mystery of life-death and thought I had lost everything. But, remarkably, my grasp loosened and I rediscovered everything in a new way. Life was everywhere, in the midst of death, even as life slipped away from me. I was able to accept that I would not experience everything in life. Actually, that there would be a whole lot that I would not experience, because I stood at the beginning—I had just turned nineteen. But somehow that no longer bothered me. Nothing was necessary. Everything became gift. Especially the simplest things.

Very little becomes indispensable after you acquire a taste for the unity of life and death. Then, as I experienced, it's not so hard to restrain yourself, to put limits on yourself. Tsimtsum then becomes almost a natural way of being. In the meantime, contrary to my expectations and those of my physicians, my life has taken another turn. For some incomprehensible reason my illness has stabilized. I am again connected to life with a thousand threads, and the hunger has come back in many ways. But something in me remains convinced of the importance of this exercise in letting go, the use of self-restraint, the imposition of self-limitation. Something in me cannot and does not want to forget how little we actually need in order to be happy. It seems to me that we could more easily respond to the urgent call of "self-restraint for the sake of the earth and those who come after us," if, individually and culturally, we learn to entrust ourselves again to the unity of life and death.

room for the unfamiliar

What is loved,
ceases to be dangerous.

Egied van Broeckhoven

The sculpture *The Kiss* by Romanian artist Brancusi has a history rich in sentiment. Brancusi created *The Kiss* in 1910. It is a beautiful work that reflects his pursuit of minimalism. It represents the essential forms of two people, while retaining the original cubic form of the raw material. You see a man and a woman, in a tight embrace. The passion is tangible. The connection palpable. Nothing can separate these two. Twenty-five years later Brancusi was commissioned to create a memorial for soldiers killed in action. Again he used *The Kiss.* Except that it became a gate. With, on the frieze, *The Kiss* repeated many times in relief, and underneath it a large opening. The love is as powerful as before, the desire for oneness still just as strong. But life created an opening . . . open to love and pain, to life and death, to what is familiar and what is strange. The theme of *The Gate of the Kiss* is "love and community." As if love that closes in on itself becomes deadly and love that opens up gives life . . .

Recently I watched a documentary featuring Cyrille Vael, a monk of Chevetogne Abbey, about the icon of the Trinity. Just like *The Kiss* of Brancusi, the icon deals with the unfamiliar that appears unexpectedly and that commands us to openness. I did not know it, but the icon of the Trinity is called "filoxenia" (hospitality) in the Orthodox Church. It harkens back to the Old Testament story of Abraham and Sarah who, seated under the oak of Mamre, receive three strangers. For those who don't know the story: Abraham and Sarah are a couple worn down by life. They had cherished big dreams and had to absorb deep disappointments. They had become realistic and gentle. They still can laugh but without exuberance. Then, unexpectedly, they become fertile. And the key, the story seems to suggest, is their openness and hospitality toward the three strangers who came calling.

"How can it be that entertaining strangers would make one fertile?" asked the interviewer. I was struck by the answer of Cyrille Vael: "The stranger is the other, that which you are not. We need the other to heal ourselves." With a smile, he added: "Otherwise you don't get any further. Without the other you remain stuck in your own little world. You settle into your self-sufficiency." Only the other breaks us open and allows us to become big of heart. Only the unfamiliar heals us of loneliness and blindness. According to Cyrille Vael the entire Bible is anchored in this notion. We are Abraham and Sarah. We need to step out of ourselves. Not once, but each and every day, even each and every minute. If not, life dries up, becomes infertile, dies.

Room for the unfamiliar . . . it sounds self-evident and seems easy, but it certainly is not. Nothing is harder. Don't we ever so quickly experience the other as a threat? We may be able to accept the distant stranger—as long as he remains sufficiently far away. But the concrete other, the person next to us, that is something else. Just think of Cain and Abel. Cain does not kill some faraway stranger. He kills his brother because his brother constitutes a threat. We don't go around killing people, but don't we use a gigantic bag of tricks to get those around us to do our bidding? Don't we continually try to talk others into playing *our* game, under *our* rules? In my experience it's far from simple to break loose from that and to let the other really be other.

Curiously, for me silence creates space for the unfamiliar. Silence unglues you from your own little world and wishes. I know this sounds like a paradox. From the outside it looks like you, just you on your meditation mat, withdraw into yourself. But it isn't that way or, rather, that's not how I experience it. It is precisely in the silence that you unhook from your own self. You become distanced from yourself. And that creates space for something other than you. Granted, at first the silence throws people back onto themselves, and that can be a trap. But in a sustained stillness the movement toward the other direction happens sooner or later. A lengthy silence always impels toward the other, the unknown, the unfamiliar.

Sometimes I think that we experience the other as a threat because we are afraid—consciously or unconsciously—of the unfamiliar in ourselves. To recognize the unfamiliar in your self is no easy matter. Recently I read *An Ordinary Life* by the Czech author Karel Čapek, a novel that deals with this. The book opens with an old man on his knees in the garden, pulling weeds from flowering boughs. Two steps away a little finch is resting on a rock, its head tilted. Out of one eye it looks at the man: who *are* you? The man finds himself face to face, perhaps for the first time ever, with the unfamiliar. It causes him to look back on his life, and he decides to write his memoir. Even though he relates the less appealing aspects of his personality and honestly talks about his acts of cowardice as a young man, the general picture that emerges is one of a good life. An ordinary existence, to be sure, but altogether the well-lived life of a functionary with the railways. But then he reviews his memoir. He notices all kinds of ambiguities and things that don't add up. All of a sudden, unfamiliarity stares him in the face from all directions. It appears that his life was complicated, full of contradictions, and had evolved very differently than he had realized. In the second part of the novel the old man touchingly learns, by trial and error, to embrace the unfamiliar in himself.

Shestov too deals with "the unfamiliar" in ourselves. "The human heart is a dark abyss," he writes, "and it requires courage to look without fear into the depths that appear bottomless to the untrained eye." Also for me, to meditate, to search out the silence, means learning to peer into the depths of my own heart without fear, becoming aware of the unfamiliar in myself, and embracing it. If we do that, then perhaps one day we will be able to cherish the unfamiliar around us . . . the strangeness of the other, the strangeness of life, the otherness of cultures, religions, and worldviews.

When I look around me and see the diversity of trees, flowers, plants, animals, and landscapes, it surprises me that we have so much difficulty in our world to make room for the unfamiliar. It looks like we always want to reduce life to *one* truth. Our truth. It's so ingrained in us to want to make everything uniform. Whether that uniformity gets labeled Zen, or Christianity, or Western culture, or something else altogether, it doesn't matter. The fact is that we forget that we can be nourished by many things. The fact is that we always want to erect dams around the rich, multibranched river of life.

Our preference, apparently, is for a navigable canal built with our own hands. As long as it brings us from point A to point B within familiar banks. The course has been set. The purpose of the voyage is known. We travel on that small, safe body of water and imagine we are on our life's journey, indeed the ultimate journey. But the ocean, with its wild currents and countercurrents, with its unknown depths and powers, we tremble at the thought. That is the unfamiliar, and we prefer not to take a chance with it. You may know where you start but not where you'll end up. In the midst of the ocean, the complete unknown beckons from every side. The ocean—no, thank you, I'd rather not.

But, really, this is odd. When we look around us, doesn't the unknown beckon everywhere? Don't we see how deeply life is marked by a multicolored variety of different ways of being? Is the visible world not one song of praise for diversity? Why aren't we stimulated by the multiplicity that comes to us from everywhere? Why is it so hard for us to take a chance with the otherness of the other, faraway and close by?

Each person, each culture, opens up a new, still unknown world. Each person, each culture, adds something new to the infinite revelation that is Life. I don't think that we are called to repeat what is known. We are called to bring to the fore the unfamiliar in our own being and to add something new to life.

To me, to love God is to love life, in all its diversity. It means to open myself up to the otherness of people and things, to try to respect that, to accept it, to learn something from it—even to feel affection for it. It also means: to tolerate the unfamiliar in people and in life. To bear it patiently without becoming embittered by it. And sometimes it means: to come up against the wall of my inability to accept this otherness. At times, to love can also be a terrible challenge for me. Experiencing inability hurts. Yet this is not just a negative thing. It also presents an opportunity to discover how the totally unfamiliar operates. Our inability to love reveals that we cannot do without that Other. It's precisely our failings that bend us, as André Louf says, to the all-encompassing total Other right in our midst, a saving presence. The unfamiliar *par excellence.*

If with our love we reach for what we know, can do, understand, cherish, can we really speak of love? Perhaps yes. Let it be "young" love. It's embracing life, in a close intertwining, as in the first *Kiss* of Brancusi. That is beautiful and meaningful, but as far as I'm concerned, that is not where the real challenge lies. To my mind, love reaches infinitely farther, toward the other, the unfamiliar, the unknown. Love that is purified and mature learns to embrace like an open gate: open wide to life in all its unfamiliarity and diversity.

up to here and not farther?

Once the people had grown tall
and
almighty,
after waiting a long time,
they found God,
numb with cold on the ground somewhere in the dark.
Well well God, they said, you here . . .
They shook their heads.
But not long after they strewed bread,
set out wine for him in saucers
and saw
how he hesitantly
came closer,
and very carefully, with one finger,
they touched him.

Toon Tellegen

February. It is still early morning as we drive through the wide, quiet, untouched landscape. The sun shines, and I enjoy it thoroughly. We stop at an immense structure that I've never visited before. To get inside is quite a job: you have to announce yourself, surrender your identity card. Next your picture is taken and tacked with a number on your coat. Then it's waiting and more waiting, until somebody comes to get you. Finally, an escort shows up. A heavy door opens and locks immediately behind us. One by one we squeeze through a narrow corridor—a detector, I notice in passing—where we have to hand over the few things we have on us. Everything is suspect here: a cell phone, a purse, even your belt. After being searched, you start a long trek through bare corridors. The low ceilings cause you to step with trepidation. Once in a while there is a halt because for the umpteenth time you have to pass through a locked door. I find it desolate and thoroughly depressing. Here and there I notice an attempt to break through that desolation. But the photographs and a handful of artful silhouettes ("Who am I?" in several languages) fail to hide the aridity of the walls. There is a stale smell, and I start feeling oppressed: no window anywhere with a clear view to the outside. And especially: nowhere a tree or a flower. Only at the entrance there was a patch of dull grass between dreary walls, behind yellowish glass that hurts the eyes. The trek ends in a black space without windows. When our eyes get accustomed to the darkness, I realize it is a chapel. Taken by surprise and a bit confused, we are left alone. It's waiting, once again, until a few of the detainees are brought from their cells. We are in the heart of the prison of Bruges.

That black space is indeed the *heart* of the prison because it's the only place where the detainees may enter without a guard. In fact, it is the only place where they can talk freely, without fear that their words will be used against them. Every two weeks, five of us from outside and five prisoners withdraw into this dark heart to talk. We talk about beautiful and difficult moments in our lives, about things we deem important, etc. These conversations were started at the request of the prison chaplains, terrific men each one of them. A drop in the bucket, but at least an attempt to break through the isolation of the inmates: there is no greater black hole of oblivion than a prison. Especially if you are serving a long sentence. You are left with nothing and nobody. Except if you're lucky enough to still have your mother . . .

The first time we worked with large black-and-white photographs. Each person selects a few to say something about himself. One man in his early thirties (he received thirty years of which he had already served seven) raises a picture of seagulls. He used to live in the countryside where he took care of animals, and he misses that. It has been years since he's seen an animal. Except for one seagull, a single time, when he was allowed to walk in open air for an hour. He is happy to see the seagulls. They move him. A twentysomething shows a photo of a car junkyard: "That kind of resembles my life." He laughs dryly. "But among that junk there are still useable parts, and I hope to do something with them once I'm out." The young man next to me says nothing. When I address him he says that he's on drugs, and he doesn't see why or for whom he should kick the habit.

It is a shocking confrontation: the aridity and depressing atmosphere of the buildings, the absence of greenery, natural beauty, homeyness. From the prisoners you hear still other things, such as uncertainty, lack of prospects, ignorance of what is going to happen next. But also how tough it can be among the lot of them, and how the days crawl by with insufferable monotony if you sit by yourself in your cell for twenty-three hours with only a television. I hear them complain about the lack of human contact, work, and income—and without money you're nothing. But worst of all, they say, is the fact that you depend on rules and the goodwill of others for everything. For example, one man told us that his best friend was dying, and that by law he had the right to go say his goodbyes. It took a month, however, before his papers were in order, and in the meantime his friend had passed away.

On the way back I cannot say that I enjoy the sun and the open landscape. Shreds of conversation amass in my head into threatening storm clouds. Soon after I am pelted with question after question: Who are they? Who am I? Where to draw the line between good and evil? What is human and what is not? Why is it that we mainly see the underprivileged and foreigners in these grey prison uniforms? Is there a connection, then, between poverty and the odds of imprisonment? I don't want to be naive. These men are no milquetoasts. What they did, I don't know. But they committed serious crimes, otherwise you don't get thirty years. I also realize that you cannot solve these kinds of things with a couple of kind words. Does that warrant placing people in isolation in bleak prisons and, when set free, in situations without hope? Who becomes a better person that way?

Shortly afterward I receive a letter from a friend in which he cites the *dharma*: "The worst enemy of compassion is called sympathy. Sympathy feels so badly for that poor fellow, as if he were different from us in any way." Maybe it sounds crazy, but reading these words untangled my jumble of thoughts and questions. Something of a fresh, fundamental simplicity appeared: whatever you try or do, what matters is compassion. And compassion is: understanding with your whole heart that the other, even if that other is an inmate, actually is no different from you. We are all cut from the same cloth. The good that a person is capable of, it also resides in them. Whatever evil they commit, it exists in us just the same. The line between good and evil runs straight through our heart. We all are and remain an awkward mixture of good and evil. We all need to be allowed to start over. Compassion truly is something else than sympathy. As long as we "feel so badly for that poor fellow," we are not on the right wavelength of compassion or, rather, compassion cannot touch us. Compassion is the big unknown, and it requires silence, a lot of silence, if it is to have a chance among us. An inner conversion needs to take place. As abbot Remi Heyse put it: "Things have to be turned upside down, all these values and certainties we suffocate ourselves and each other with. And then we discover that it's not the things that are upside down, but *we* who have lived our whole life *upside down*."

This reminds me of a story told by Toon Tellegen. It's about a squirrel who, one day, draws a line in the sand along the riverbank and who remains on one side of the line. Up to here, and not farther, he says to himself. For a long time he had intended to draw such a line and not to cross it. At least then I know my place, he thought. He was tired and sat down, and looked at the other side of the line. It looked as if everything was different there. But he had a hard time making out *what* was different. At a given moment, he hears the cricket calling. "Oh," he says, "you are at the wrong side of the line. I can't join you." He hears the cricket say: "Then I'll eat it all by myself." Now the squirrel is so full of curiosity that he looks around to make sure nobody sees him and then, quickly, with his tail, he erases the line. Maybe it's not quite such a good thing to know where you're at. But when he reaches the cricket, it's too late. The beechnut is finished. The squirrel's shoulders droop and he slouches back home in the dusk. He promised himself never again to draw a line to know his place.

The unknown only gets a chance if we dare erase the lines we draw. As long as we don't do that and remain standing on one side of the line, what is essential passes us by. It's a paradox. Because it is a human reflex to draw lines. We do it continually, and it is necessary. We cannot do otherwise. For society to be livable, there have to be limits to what can and cannot be done. Up to here. And not farther. But in life, doesn't a call always ring out from behind the line as well?

stretched out in the grass

somewhere it has to exist
some sort of overgrown garden
of ancient silence

the tree in front of the house
softly whispers its tale
that nobody understands

it has rained
the garden steams good smells
the earth is yearning.

J. C. van Schagen

25th Hour. A Spike Lee movie. The story takes place in New York. Another twenty-four hours before Monty Brogan has to enter prison for seven years. He dealt drugs, somebody squealed on him. Monty passes the evening with his dad. When night falls, in the twilight of a local nightclub and the company of two old buddies, he starts wrestling with the angels and the demons of his life. You see him tossed around by rage, sorrow, his fear of America's prisons, and acceptance. I watched *25th Hour* as part of a spiritual movie event. A confrontation with human- and world perspectives of unbelievers, Buddhists, and Christians. A trialogue, with images as the foundation.

One of the lasting images from this Spike Lee movie is the tirade in front of the mirror. Monty's struggle with his conscience (to flee or to pay for his crimes) explodes when he's standing alone in front of the mirror in the men's room. He slams just about every population group that comes into his head. One by one, people parade in the mirror: New Yorkers, hard-working people, losers, fathers and mothers, immigrants, children, and so on. It's a volley of insults that is also a tribute to the multicultural metropolis. It ends when Monty realizes that he can't blame anybody for his (mis)deeds but himself.

Another fragment that stays with you comes at the end of the movie. Father and son are driving through a panoramic landscape. On the run or to prison? The movie leaves the question hanging. Only at the end does it become clear that the drive is indeed to the jail. The car stops. Monty and his dad get out, two paper-thin lines in the wasteland. Suddenly you hear Monty's dad say: "Once in their life, everybody should see the desert. That enormous plain. Only sand, rocks, cacti, and blue sky. Not a human being in sight. No sirens, no car alarms, no honking, no idiots that curse or piss in the street. There you find silence. There you find repose. There you can find God. The desert is a new beginning."

It is an impressive scene. The contrast between the hustle and bustle of New York City, where just about the whole movie takes place, and then suddenly, unexpectedly, this penetrating moment of silence and emptiness. The wasteland big as life on the screen and with it the question: are we not suppressing something fundamental with our big-city lifestyle? Are we not excluding on principle any possible experience of silence with our culture of busyness, tempo, and tumult? And doesn't it play us for fools? Don't we all hold tirades in front of the mirror, and without silence don't we all get stuck in our (mis)deeds in one way or another?

I read in one of Karen Armstrong's books the life story of the Buddha. How he traveled a long path of failed attempts to attain enlightenment. How no effort was too much. How he finally subjected himself to the most severe asceticism in order to annihilate his ego, that grasping, clamoring "I" that haunts us and never leaves us in peace. To no avail. Nothing helped. At his wits' end, he remembers a moment from the time he was a small boy. He was sitting in the shadow of a tree. Alone. He looked around and was suddenly touched by the suffering of the grass and some insects. It awoke a deep compassion in him and an inexpressible joy. He realizes that there, under that tree, he had spontaneously achieved what he so ardently desired. Just like that, without the least effort.

The beautiful thing is that he starts reflecting on that experience: how was it possible? Digging in his memory he finds that the chambermaids who were to keep an eye on him had left him alone, against his father's wishes. He realizes that he would never have encountered that rich experience but for his aloneness. He simply would not have had a chance. The afternoon would have been filled with chatter about this and that. That's just how people behave when in company. It reminds me of Rilke, who writes somewhere that one day, touched by one thing or another, he did not wish to join others. What moved him so dearly in silence would inevitably be lost—he sensed intuitively—in the din of people's interactions.

Both anecdotes, about the Buddha and Rilke, are suggestive of the invaluable importance of silence. There is an understanding of everything that is of the utmost importance for this world and this life, but it cannot happen without some kind of dying born out of silence. That kind of understanding is alive and inexpressible. A nothing that reveals everything . . . But in order to discover it we must keep our distance from chatter and noise. We must dare to stand in our solitude and become very still. And that requires courage. It is dying a little.

My illness pushed me into a horrible isolation and left me with a choice. It was a matter of bending (and becoming deeply still) or breaking. And so it remains: bending or breaking. And perhaps a part of us needs to break before we are able to bend and to become deeply still. Perhaps it is not by chance that the silence in *25th Hour* appears only at the end of the movie. The comforting, refreshing, all-restoring silence, I mean. The silence that topples one's perspective on everything.

Because in a certain way, the whole movie is pervaded by silence. Albeit a loaded, negative silence. The stillness of a life that literally comes to a "standstill." In *25th Hour*, Spike Lee knows how to prolong time. He incorporates many tranquil scenes. At one point in the nightclub he even completely stops the sound. You see everybody dancing and jumping, while an icy silence reigns. Then the camera zooms in on Monty, who sits by himself on a bench amid all that tumult without sound. This is masterful. It expresses exactly what happens when you are confronted with something serious. You can actually see and hear everything around you. At the same time, you find yourself in some sort of isolation. In the middle of everything and everybody, it appears that you are secluded from your surroundings. What kind of struggle with angels and demons takes place in us at such moments, before we surrender and, exhausted, allow ourselves to fall into the silence . . . toward an unknown and unexpected freedom?

Kierkegaard also refers to the inestimable importance of quieting ourselves. I read once a sublime reflection of his on "the lilies in the field" from the Gospel according to Matthew. The lily in the field is one of his metaphors for what cannot be expressed. We are that lily. We are planted in life and have to wait for spring. But can we summon enough patience to wait? Are we sufficiently quiet and silent to recognize the moment of spring? Do we dare to make time during which we keep a distance from all chatter so that we notice the instant spring happens and are able to seize it? He writes:

> The lily does not ask impatiently when spring will finally arrive. When the moment comes, the silent lily understands that this is *the* moment and she knows how to

> use it. Oh, you dainty, thoughtful masters of simplicity, who know that we can never catch the moment while we talk. No, the moment only speaks when there is no speech and if even only one word is uttered it is lost. That's why it happens so rarely that a person properly understands when the instant has arrived: it's because he cannot keep his mouth shut. With all the talking he did not even notice that the moment had appeared. Even though the instant may be pregnant with meaning, it does not send a messenger ahead to announce its arrival: the moment is too sudden for that when it arrives. Also, the instant does not arrive with noise and shouts, no matter how rich in significance it may be. No, it arrives softly, on the light feet of the sudden. That's why we have to be very quiet if we wish to notice "that it's here now." Because the next moment, it's totally gone. That's why we have to be completely silent if we want to make the most of it. Indeed, everything depends on the instant. But the unfortunate thing is that most people never perceive it, with the result that during their whole life, time and eternity remain split. And why? Because they were unable to be silent.

Then do we have to pass through winter before we are able to notice spring? Something in me says: Yes. Because I often see it happen. Frequently people go through a long and difficult struggle with angels and demons before they come to a real standstill and they realize with amazement that in that stillness the old perspective shifts. Nevertheless, at the same time something in me says: No. When I dig into my own memories and keep in mind the story about the Buddha in Armstrong's book, I have to admit that it is true. Just by myself as a child, stretched out in the grass under the shadow of a tree, I had discovered it spontaneously.

nobody's breath

Return to a primal happening,
to the core of the universe,
where life is forever created anew.

Louise Kleinherenbrink

A few years ago, on a splendid Indian summer day, a friend took me to see an exhibit of modern sculpture in Temse. The exhibit was entitled: *Nobody's Breath—Visual Impressions of Transcience*. Several local and international artists presented their works, which expressed their vision of the transitory nature of time. We found ourselves in an extensive garden in the valley of the Durme River, and we watched people walking from one sculpture to another. The garden was steeped in a deep quiet, and the whole scene breathed serenity and warmth. We joined the procession that advanced with slow step among the silent witnesses to the caresses and lashes of time. Wondrously, everybody respected the silence. As if we all passed through the garden in a sort of *kinhin* (walking meditation), paying attention to our breath. Nobody's breath. That title alone! This was profoundly touching art. And it struck me that, in a time of fashionable nihilism, there are still artists who dare to go deep.

It reminds me of two women: Els Vermandere and Louise Kleinherenbrink. Their art is precious to me precisely because it is so moving. Els is a sculptress. She works principally with Burgundian whitestone. One cannot help but be affected by her statues. It is as if they sing in the rhythm of deeper strings, as if they dance to the rhythm of a larger song. In her hands stone turns into poetry. She kneads roughness into tenderness and cleaves hardness into peace. The statues invite us to keep watch over that which is precious within us.

Louise is a painter. Two of her paintings remain with me as if they were burned into my retinas. They both play on the theme of unconditional love and how that love moves boundaries. The first is *The Compassion of Kwan Yin*, in which Kwan Yin, the Bodhisattva of Infinite Compassion, offers her help in the figure of a prostitute. The second is called *The Mother of Judas.* The painting depicts a woman, nearly nude, vulnerable. The face of Judas is imprinted on her shirt, like the face of Jesus on Veronica's veil. She is weighted down by the burden of the centuries-old judgment of her son. But in her arms, almost hidden, she nourishes a great love for her child. About this last painting, Louise herself says: "Often I have asked myself how it would be if I had been this mother, or if I had been Judas. Then I realize how safe my world is, where I have never had to face these choices."

At one of the poetry summers in Watou, Louise and I stood in front of a piece of sculpture that stood out in its absurdity. I don't remember what exactly Louise said at the time. But, basically, it struck her as despondency for despondency's sake, coming from somebody who clearly had never suffered in life. At one time Els had said something similar. The conversation had to do with the process of searching and a society that fails to encourage this in any way. We talked about art, literature, and poetry, and the penchant for fashions in these fields. We spoke of how it can be so devoid of content, and that there is a certain cowardice in that.

The conversations with these two women warmed my heart. I enjoy modern art, but at times even I find its nihilism cheap. Not that art is not allowed to be raw or shocking. That actually seems important to me and it can move me deeply. In that sense I can appreciate nihilism in art. When as an artist you endeavor to show the absurdities of life, I'm with you. When, however, these absurdities lead to something nearly like a cheerful feeling, that goes a bit too far. That I can't stomach. Then you have a despondency that retains complete freedom, just to please a handful of trendsetters. It's despondency *de luxe*. And all the while life goes on very nicely, no problem at all. Nihilism with a smiling face. It simply doesn't compute. Forgotten in all of this is that art always makes an impression—positively or negatively, but art *does* do something. Words and statues are never neutral. If as an artist you are oblivious to the impact of your words and images on possible readers or viewers, then you have not yet suffered in life—you are lacking something.

How different is the attitude of these two women and the artists in Temse. Louise Kleinherenbrink expresses it aptly: "No matter how briefly we are engaged with art, it is always a contribution to life. It is an effort to take our own unique place and to express that uniqueness. In lieu of bringing about destruction, each one of us can create this kind of reality, one that grows and that continues to create new life."

It strikes me that artists sometimes have a sense of something that resembles responsibility. In Jacqueline Harpman's novel *The Beach of Ostend* [*Het strand van Oostende*] the artist Leopold Wiesbeck says that he decided to devote himself to painting in the same way that somebody resolves to enter the convent. To be so stirred, to feel such responsibility! This is art as devotion, art as something of existential importance for the artist as well as for the viewer.

Marguerite Yourcenar once said in an interview: "If my books have helped only one person along in this life, then I feel my writing is a success." What a great good fortune it is that some writers and artists are conscious of the fact that their words and images can truly save people. I still remember how I, in the difficult period of falling ill and failing to envision any kind of future, was literally "caught" by a centuries-old, tiny statuette. It still stands in my cabinet, in the place where I meditate. It is my Kwan Yin . . .

It happened in Greece, in the Museum of Cycladian Art in Athens. I went there with my sister and a friend in hopes of finding solace for the torture that had become my life. Greece was the only place that came to mind. Probably because at that time it was the most familiar to me. I had greatly enjoyed studying Greek in high school, and I wanted to see what was left of that culture. In any event, I ended up in Athens, in the Museum of Cycladian Art, amid a sea of small, white-marble statuettes. The figures had a simplicity that touched me right away. They appeared modern and their features veered toward the abstract, even though they were produced between 4,000 and 1,100 BC. Most of them represented women's figures, without face, for use in the cult of the God Mother.

I became totally captivated by these "urmothers." One of the figurines represented a woman's figure that was all hunched up. It awoke something like a primeval realization in me: if nothing is clear anymore, the only thing left is to look into yourself. Without words, and without my realizing it, this age-old statuette made me take the first steps into myself. This piece of art from times long past, from a totally different culture, worked a change in me that neither I myself nor those around me had been able to accomplish. It is as if art can communicate where words and people fail. This little, ancient statue pulled me out of my isolation. It got me moving, perhaps because it contained a primeval sadness and a primeval desire. In any case, it represented something with which I felt a close affinity. There in Athens I became aware for the first time that death is something that you can rise up from. For an instant, something buoyed up in me. For once I liked the tourist shops! I could not have cared less that the reproduction was only so-so. I bought the statuette. Later I would have to go through hell. But no matter. A glimmer of light made a mighty difference in a night that was black as coal.

I have often experienced the importance of art, even if not always as acutely as that time in Athens. Some things are too large and others too small for words. It does not always have to be about sorrow—joy, too, can surpass the power of words. Fortunately for us there is something like the wordless language of sculpture. What cannot be spoken still wants to be said. Bliss, as well as the sadness beyond all words, also wants to be expressed.

Art is of existential importance for me. It is something that I consciously surround myself with. Not only by attending galleries but also by having it at home. Every morning I draw sustenance from Els Vermandere's statue in the hall cabinet. Every day I lose myself for a while in the abstract-figurative paintings of Dirk Verhulst and Karin van der Molen that hang on the wall of our living room. Every evening my last regard goes to a piece of art by Nicole Huijs-Karrèr that symbolizes the imperfect body. Don't ask why they move me. It has to do with something beyond words. I only know that I could not do without them. Without this kind of fine art my life would be a shadow of what it is now. Without it, bitterness would gain the upper hand. These art pieces enable something. They keep something open and supple. They are as necessary to me as silence. Or perhaps I should put it another way: for me they *are* a form of silence—in contrast to the grasping confusion of this or that kind of art that is the fashion of the day. In real art there is always a taste of stillness, I think. Is it a coincidence that all the artists I know enjoy the company of silence?

troublesome companions

Fear is the heartbeat
of impotence.

Cor de Jonghe

Sadness, anger, fear. Three daily companions on the journey of a debilitating illness. Impossible to avoid this threesome. Early in the morning, long before I get up, they're already there. At night, long after I go to bed, they do not budge. They never leave me in peace. There's no getting away from them. I have no choice but to learn to get along with these three troublesome companions, or they'll trip me up. If I'm not careful, they will pitilessly destroy the little bit of *joie de vivre* that remains in my life.

You can manage with sadness. It accumulates, and when the bucket is full, you have tears that you can freely let go. Nothing is as liberating as a good cry.

With anger you can also manage, albeit somewhat less easily. Anger you can vent. That clears the air markedly, and there are a thousand ways to let off steam. But I hardly know a way that is tolerable for those around you. Especially if you are ill and dependent on others. Nevertheless, anger has the advantage that, like sadness, it can be expressed.

But how do you deal with fear?

Fear you can only suffer. When you are in the grip of fear, it paralyzes you, and you see no way out. Fear reduces you to complete impotence, and there is nothing you can do to lighten it. It's an emotion that is impossible to vent or to take out on somebody or something. The only thing you can do is wait—until the fear recedes on its own. That's why fear is the worst thing that can happen to a person.

live your questions now

High in the sky hung a question mark.
Why?
People climbed on each other's shoulders
and took a close look.
It's an ancient exclamation mark, they said,
it's warped,
it nearly collapses.

They decided to devote the rest of their lives
to the meaning of this thing.

They proceeded on their path,
passed quotation marks,
footnotes and slips of the pen,
parentheses were opened
and promptly closed
and in the distance discerned three periods
. . .
in the bright white of immortality.

Toon Tellegen

When I lost my balance for the umpteenth time due to lack of strength in my arms, I hit the ground with a bang. I was rushed to the hospital in an ambulance, my head heavily bandaged because they feared a cranial fracture or internal bleeding. And I sensed again, with razor-sharpness, how uncertain life actually is. In an ambulance you are not just literally banged around, your soul also gets shook up. Even if the drive is short, it's always long enough to realize with dismay how, face to face with the fragility of life, not much remains of our elegant theories. Instantly, all our exclamation marks about life vanish. They warp and become the question that Toon Tellegen writes about with such insistence. Not so much the question "why me?" but "why?" Whether it is me who has to suffer or somebody else, that doesn't matter. There is insufferable pain in the world and that provokes protest: why? The question is not only very painful but also, even more, it is impossible, because there is no answer to it.

As long as your life runs smoothly, you can ignore the question and go on living. When you encounter a mishap, things change. Boom, there is that question, in all its impossibility. You don't see a way out. You face a wall. When life sticks you with a wall, everybody is quick to explain it or to make it relative. From religion to science, the experts have ready explanations. But as far as I was concerned, the question remained. They could all go to hell with their explanations. When pain cuts raw into your skin, any explanation of it is unbearable. All the so-called knowledge of science and religion enraged me. Yet I did not want to descend into nihilism. How does one manage to reconcile that?

The paradox is that liberation can begin when we allow that painful and impossible question into our life. "The big questions of life have to find shelter somewhere," writes Etty Hillesum. Liberation is only possible if you shelter that question within and take it with you into the silence—weeks, months, years if need be, even if it looks at first like the ground disappears from under your feet. The paradox is that this difficult, mysterious bottomlessness is actually something you can stand on. But the way to discover that is long and the price is high.

In Zen practice, one does not avoid confrontation with the impossible question of existence. One who travels the path of Zen is encouraged to *sit* with it, literally. It's called "practicing with a *koan*." It is a fundamental practice in Zen Buddhism. Originally *koans* were testimonies to an existential impasse and the subsequent liberation. It's all about using these texts to obtain insight into the impossible question, the impasse, or the wall in our own lives. A *koan*—the literal translation of *koan* is "impossible question"—aims at removing the familiar ground on which we stand and challenging us to take a liberating step.

That impossible question figures far more prominently and insistently in our lives than we are willing to recognize. I was confronted with it well before I fell ill and my life turned into a drama. In so many novels I read the question. I hear it in so many stories that people tell. All variations on the same basic theme. Apparently it's the question that we all keep returning to.

I first became aware of this during lectures in psychoanalysis at the University of Leuven. Psychoanalysts like Lacan call that impossible question "a gap in the center of human desire." When I heard that, it really struck me. We are creatures of desire, but in the center of that desire yawns a void, and that void cannot be filled by anything or anybody. Even stronger: it's exactly that emptiness that is the engine of all longing. Without it our desire is dead. French psychoanalyst Françoise Dolto has a beautiful image to render this impossibility that exists in the center of human longing. She refers to an old-fashioned letter game made up of a plastic square containing a bunch of letters that you have to move around to form a word. The whole game revolves around an empty square in between the letters. What a metaphor! We are all looking for something in life. We probe and move around, searching for meaning. But whatever we do or try, there always remains an emptiness, and sooner or later that becomes an impasse, a wall. "Don't be surprised that the wall without gate is so difficult and that it arouses *intense anger*," says *Wu-men kuan* (*Wall without Gates*), a well-known compendium of *koans* from the eleventh century.

I can say a thing or two about that wall without gate and the anger it arouses. At the beginning of my illness, the fact that my situation held no future made me enormously angry. I fumed with rage. For months on end. My whole being rebelled. Later a Catholic priest told me that there can be no resurrection without insurrection. Later still, during Zen retreats, I heard touching testimonies about the impossible to understand link between rebellion—especially against God—silence, and faith against all odds. But at that time, there was no question of resurrection. Only of fierce insurrection.

In those days I was ignorant of *koans*. I needed Rilke to widen my perspective and to get me on my way. According to Rilke, the point is not to look for answers but *to live* the questions. In his *Letters to a Young Poet*, he encourages young Kappus to have patience with all the unresolved matters in his heart and "to try to love the *questions themselves* like locked rooms and like books that are written in a very foreign tongue." He writes: "Do not now seek the answers, which cannot be given you, because you would not be able to live them. And the point is, to live everything. *Live* the questions now. Perhaps you will then gradually, without noticing it, live along some distant day into the answer."

I read a lot at that time. I kept a notebook in which I recorded passages that touched me, including these words of Rilke. I still smile at this colorful collection of thoughts from all possible sources. I was not looking for anything in particular. My only criterion was: does it move me? I picked up thoughts everywhere, from poets and writers but also from singers and mystics. I even plucked them from billboards and the cardboard coasters that we put our beer glasses on in pubs. I remember the bright blue poster that a girlfriend had hung in her apartment when she went to live by herself and barely had anything. It read: "I possess nothing, but I am." Upon returning home, sentences like that went right into my notebook. They were small stepping stones that laid a path upon the waves. Without these stepping stones, the stormy sea would have swallowed me. But the words remained. Always. If I can recommend anything, it is this: read, prick up your ears, use your eyes, and write down what moves you. It's your best guide. At that time, I did not realize this. But now, looking back, I realize that each word came at exactly the right time and that it was exactly the word I needed at that moment. These are things that make you sit back and feel grateful.

Thus, Rilke taught me to experience the questions rather than just to reflect on them. Does life become a question mark? Does it call for rebellion? Then *live* that question. *Live* the rebellion. Maybe then, little by little, without becoming aware of it, you will begin to *live* the answer. Rilke is convinced that this answer, just like any kind of progress, must come from *deep inside* and cannot be hurried or hastened by anything. He taught me to go and sit with the impossible question of existence and "to await, in humility and with patience, the birthing of a new clarity." His attitude of staying with the question without lapsing into nihilism touched me deeply, and still does. It bespeaks confidence, and a great faith. "To mature," he writes, "as the tree that does not pump up its sap and quietly endures the springtime showers without fear that there will be no summer to follow. Summer comes anyway."

What happens when you act that way can hardly be put into words. An answer arrives, from deep inside, beyond all words and images. You are touching on what cannot be expressed and are being filled with a "not-knowing knowing," as Eckhart puts it. If you wait in silence, in confidence, even if inside of you a storm rages and screams and the ground disappears from under your feet, then what happens to you is what happened to Job: the tears of rebellion, anger, and despair change into tears of quiet emotion, and that is a great miracle. In the psalms and the old monastic books this is called "contrition of the heart." It is an expression that has always moved me. Monks know that "*un coeur blessé est un coeur ouvert*," a broken heart is an open heart. It is odd, but that's the way it is. That brokenness opens us up.

the one seat

For wisdom is more mobile than any motion;
because of her pureness she pervades
and penetrates all things.

The Wisdom of Solomon 7:24

What is wisdom? An eternal question for me. Apparently also for Benoît Standaert, a Benedictine monk in the city of Bruges. He devoted a number of lectures to it, based on the Old Testament Wisdom books. In his view, the first step on the path of wisdom is to obtain broad knowledge and background. This demands a willingness to become immersed in more than one wisdom tradition. In other words, wisdom starts with breadth. You have to be ready to expand your horizons. If that is the beginning of wisdom, I'm ready to listen. You often hear the opposite when people start talking about their own tradition: a wariness and mistrust of everything that is foreign to their own background.

My sense is that Benoît Standaert is saying something profound. Without a dimension of breadth there is no wisdom. It reminds me of a beautiful passage in Simone Weil that is right on point. I hit upon it while reading her little book *Waiting for God*. She writes: "My thought should be indifferent to all ideas without exception, including for instance materialism and atheism; it must be equally welcoming and equally reserved with regard to every one of them. Water is indifferent in this way to the objects that fall into it. It does not weigh them; they weigh themselves, after a certain time of oscillation."

Wisdom starts by "having no preference." She presupposes an attitude of receptivity. Just as water welcomes everything that falls in it. It is a blessing of our time that we can be receptive to anything and everything. We have easy access to all kinds of spiritual sources. I am thinking of the great classic book of Taoism that was recently translated into Dutch: *Zhuang Zi: The Complete Works* [*Zhuang Zi. De volledige geschriften*]. Or *The Writings of Liezi* [*De geschriften van Liezi*] about the Tao's ability to put things in perspective. Until recently, you had to be a specialist to have an opportunity to immerse yourself in texts like these. Nowadays treasures like these can be readily snatched up in bookstores and libraries. I found the writings of Zhuang Zi in our modest village library, on the "warmly recommended" table.

This "breadth dimension" hits me whenever we sing the sutra of Kwan Yin in the Maha Karuna Ch'an. Kwan Yin personifies unconditional compassion. She descends into hell to save each and every one, without exception. The sutra is an ode to that redemption. First there is a song about how the heart cry that reaches Kwan Yin brings relief to the suffering person. In the sutra's second part follows a remarkable enumeration of the saving forms that Kwan Yin assumes, and it is the breadth of that enumeration that moves me. The sutra mentions just about everything under the sun. It says: "If somebody can be saved by a Buddha or a bodhisattva, by a child or a senior, by the Christian Redeemer or the Mother of God, by Yahweh's suffering servant or the Shekinah of Jewish mysticism, by a wise man of Islam or a Sufi, by a god or goddess of Hinduism, by a convinced atheist, by those who are complete failures . . . then she will take on that form."

It appears that the Kwan Yin sutra, as sung in the Maha Karuna Ch'an, believes that you can be a Muslim with the Muslims, a Buddhist with the Buddhists, a Christian with the

Christians, and an atheist with the atheists. I find that very moving. It evinces an unimaginable wisdom and depth. I don't believe that one can share that deep experience without a modicum of knowledge about Islam, Buddhism, Christianity, and atheism. At the same time, something more is required. Breadth of knowledge is insufficient by itself. Another dimension is necessary: somehow you also need to be in touch with something in depth. Wisdom has two dimensions . . .

A while ago I was at the abbey of Chevetogne in the Wallonia region of Belgium. It was my first time, and I participated, also for the first time, in a Slavic-Byzantine and Greek Orthodox liturgy. It moved me greatly. Last year I went to listen to Algerian Sufi master Sheik Khaled Bentounès with a group of Muslims and Christians. It was about the prayer of the heart in Sufism. Afterward there was a moment of prayer. The Muslims who were present performed Sufi songs and that also moved me greatly. Atheists don't sing. And yet, if I read novels or other texts by atheist authors, I detect from time to time a poignant melody. Literature can be liturgy as well. "How is it possible?" I asked myself in Chevetogne. "How is it that a person can be moved by things that are so far apart?"

If I answer that question for myself in all honesty, I can only say: "Because underneath all that diversity lies one and the same depth." Indeed it is my experience that if you delve deeply enough, at a certain moment you reach a vein that courses underneath everything. No matter where you dig, if you go deep enough, you arrive at that stream; you recognize it, everywhere. It is true what is said in the Wisdom of Solomon: "Wisdom is more mobile than any motion, she pervades and penetrates all things . . ."

In order to discover this, you have to dig deeply. And: you have to dig yourself. The water that another brings up from the well does not do it. Only the water that you heist up yourself slakes your thirst. And, by the way, it does not matter where you start digging. You can start with Christianity, or with Buddhism, or somewhere else. No matter where. But if you start with a certain tradition, it means that you have to get into it in depth. Not only words but also deeds. Reading is not enough. You have to immerse yourself in something, just like walking a path. Not a little bit. No, for years.

I myself went digging in Christianity. More specifically, in monastic spirituality: the Benedictine tradition and that of the Desert Fathers. I came upon a stillness that I had never known before and upon texts that I did not know existed. I was confronted with two unfamiliar practices: the habit of monks and nuns to sing the psalms and to sit silently on a bench and pray. I found the psalms as impossible to understand as the monotone melody in which they were recited. Even stranger to me was sitting silently on a little bench. But I participated, and after a while I started doing it at home as well. That's what I mean with immersing yourself in something and devoting yourself to a path. Of course, I also read a lot about that kind of spirituality. But first and foremost for me was this: dedicating myself to the unfamiliar practice of singing psalms and sitting in silence. Benoît Standaert once told me how. When he was asked once to explain the meaning of praying the psalms, he suggested to practice it first for ten years or so. "Then we can have a talk about it," he said. Now that is digging . . .

The misfortune of most people is that they dig a little hole, and then they say to themselves: "This will come to nothing." A little later they see something that looks more alluring: "Well, let me give this a try." In this way, they dig hole after hole after hole, without ever reaching depth. In some way, it's understandable. Digging is hard work. You have to dig through a good many layers of nonsense and boredom. It requires blood, sweat, and tears. But it's the only way. Wherever people from different backgrounds find each other and really meet, you note this: they have dug deeply. Wherever people, religions, and philosophies face off against each other, you see: they remain stuck in the building of a well, busily working on the little roof on top, important things like that! But hopefully, one day they will be really digging.

Jack Kornfield, the American Buddhist meditation teacher, impressed me with his expression "take the one seat." He puts into words the same intuition, with the same image. We have to choose one place and sink a deep well there. Otherwise, transformation is impossible. He describes taking the one seat as follows: "If we satisfy ourselves with a bit of practice in one tradition, and a bit from another, and then a bit more from yet a third, the work that we do will probably not accumulate when we start on the next practice. It's like digging a number of shallow holes in lieu of a deep well. Skipping from one thing to another means that we never need to face our own boredom, impatience, and fears. In this way, we never confront ourselves."

Wisdom is cultivated by discovering and receiving much in breadth, but by going deeply into only one tradition. A true statement, yet I have not fully complied with it, and I am not sorry. Once in a while, shifting your focus is also important. On condition that you then discipline yourself to resume "your seat." I guess it's the nature of the beast. When I studied psychology, I also took courses in theology. I wanted to have a sense of how one could look at a human being's reality from a different perspective.

Becoming intimately familiar with a totally different tradition is also an enriching experience. For me, it was Zen. To my surprise, I discovered a good number of similarities: sitting in silence, recitation of texts, cultivation of certain attitudes, etc. But, to my mind, the differences are particularly enriching. Christians can learn something from the deep silence of Zen. Conversely, many Western Zen practitioners could learn from the humility and simplicity of Christian monks. You see your blind spots better in the mirror of another tradition. The sharp edges get blunted. One-dimensionality is transcended. I do not believe in a spiritual uniformity diet in which all differences are swept under the rug in order to achieve a false peace. Each tradition has its own emphases. In order to grow, we need the differences. To immerse ourselves in another tradition is like learning a second language. It is to discover that what is most important lies beyond words but that, at the same time, there are things that can only be said in that one language.

being at home with yourself

Once upon a time, long, long ago, in an orthodox abbey
there lived an old monk.
Pamve was his name.
He planted a dead tree on a mountain.
He ordered his apprentice Ivan Kolov
to water the tree every day
until it came back to life.
Every morning Ivan went on his way with a pail,
climbed the mountain and watered the dead trunk.
And in the evening after dark had fallen
he returned to the abbey.
So it went for three years in a row.
And one fine day he arrived at the top
and saw the tree in full blossom.
Say what you want, but a system has its advantages.
If every single day, at exactly the same time, you did
the identical thing—ritually, imperturbably,
systematically—
every day at exactly the same time,
the world would change.
Something changes then, irrevocably . . .

From *The Offering* [*Het offer*] by Tarkovski

Nothing is as difficult as sticking it out with yourself. Somebody who is a prisoner in his body, like me, and who consequently spends a lot of time with himself, will confirm this wholeheartedly. But I also hear the same thing from others. This is not to say that to be by yourself is always a problem. We also enjoy it. Aloneness can open you up to many things: creativity, reading, getting to the bottom of things and of yourself, being in touch with nature, etc. But there is also that other side: the challenge, the struggle. A monk once said: "Nothing makes a man toil harder than doing nothing." It can cause us to fall into an apathy that proves impossible to shake.

In monastic literature this is called the sin of *acedia* (laziness, sadness, feelings of depression). It was gratifying to read that Bernardo Olivera, the abbot general of the Trappists, also refers to the Japanese word *mu-ki-ryoku* to elucidate this condition: *mu* (lack of), *ki* (energy), *ryoku* (strength, power). He adds: "Those who are familiar with the importance of the term *ki* in Eastern cultures will understand that acedia is very serious. The listless person is exhausted, lacks energy or dynamism, and is horrified of harmony with God, with others, and with the universe." Portuguese poet Fernando Pessoa speaks in this connection of "the burden of world consciousness, an inability to breathe with the soul."

Who does not recognize this? It is not easy to be alone. It can cause serious inner struggle and doubt. Or it can cause paralysis, so that empty time becomes dead time instead of free time. I hear it so often from people, and I recognize it in myself: you have a day off, you intend to do lots of things, but suddenly you're thrown back upon yourself in an unpleasant way. A somber mood comes upon you and you can't shake it. The dark clouds remain and, unless you take care, you remain stuck in a chair, utterly disquieted yet paralyzed. Hence, many people prefer to fill up their calendars. It saves them from a difficult confrontation. But by acting that way, aren't you continually on the run? Aren't you really running away from yourself and reality? For me, this is a crucial question. The issue of sticking it out with yourself is such a stumbling block that I want to devote a separate chapter to it. I cannot write about a wonderful, dynamic way of stillness, a way *in* stillness, and keep silent about this dreadful, dead point. It would not be honest. Doubt, toil, fret, struggle, and paralysis truly are part and parcel of the ineffable process that takes place in silence.

As I look at myself and my surroundings, our days are so full that we have no time to spend with ourselves, or so empty that we don't have the strength to do it. We are so often out of the house, and if we are at home we are not at home with our own selves. The way of monks and Zen practitioners is at odds with ours. The spiritual traditions of the East and the West move in a totally different direction. Where we go out as often as we can, toward the fascinating world—and there is nothing intrinsically wrong with that—they turn inward, into themselves. They start where we end. The dead point that we would rather evade, they see as the starting point. Precisely this "being with yourself" is, in their view, of crucial importance.

To be at home with yourself (*habitare secum* in Latin) is a basic exercise in the Benedictine tradition. It means to take time every day to listen in silence to what is within you. In other words, that you insert moments during which you dwell with yourself in silence, no matter how difficult it may be. It is also a basic exercise in Zen: *zazen*, sitting in silence, "being intimate with yourself," as Zen teacher Frank De Waele calls it. It can be done in various ways: attentively following your breath, or simply observing your thoughts, impulses, mood changes . . . without making judgments. Monks sit on a bench, Zen practitioners on a meditation cushion, but basically they do the same thing: they introduce moments in which they are with themselves in silence.

We find that rather strange. Why would you apply yourself to something as silly? A waste of your time, we say. But more than anything, we find it difficult. Why endure turmoil, confusion, and gloominess, when there are so many attractive ways to escape from all that? We would rather evade silence than look for it. At least, that's the way it was and is for me. I am not exactly spontaneously drawn to go and sit on my meditation mat with my turmoil. Yet, I know, these spiritual traditions have a point. What this point is you can only discover by *doing* it yourself. It has to do with one's life fulfillment. But *what* this fulfillment contains, you can only experience by walking that path yourself.

Honesty requires me to say that I started on this difficult practice of "being and staying with yourself" for the sole reason that my means of escape no longer served. It was a school of hard knocks, but now I would not want to have missed it for any gold in the world. Even if honesty also requires me to say that it is a path of falling and picking yourself up and forever starting anew. I often have to overcome resistance to go and sit with myself on my mat, even now, after all these years. But did the Japanese Zen Master Shunryu Suzuki not say: "*Zen mind, beginner's mind*"?

It is said of Benedict that he was at home with himself. Isn't it beautiful to be able to say that of somebody? Don't you wish right away that you could meet such a person? In any event, when I heard these words, a desire was aroused in me. I wanted to learn this being at home with myself, no matter how afraid I was of it. Ever since then, I try to make time every day to be with myself in silence. Even if it is only a half hour or ten minutes. It's a way to become, and especially to stay, in touch with yourself and what is real, in a society that pulls on us from all sides. But it is also a battle. It requires courage to dwell with yourself in stillness.

If we come to a standstill, our demons get free rein, say the monks; and we don't have someplace to hide these demons or somebody on whom to pawn them off. Exterior noise is replaced by inner unrest, and that is stifling. In their eyes, it is precisely that painful confrontation that offers a way out. The art is not to run away from yourself at that moment. You have to stay "in your cell" and dare to endure the inner turmoil. Benedictine Sister Johanna Domek puts it aptly:

"Inner noise can be quite exhausting. That's probably why so many flee to the seduction of exterior background noises. They prefer to have the noise just wash over them. But if you want to grow spiritually, you have to stay inside the room of your spiritual raging and persevere. You have to continue to sit silently and honestly in God's presence, until the raging quiets down and your heart gradually becomes cleansed and quieted." Anselm Grün talks about "descending into your own reality with humility." Precisely by going down to the soil of which we are a part—*humilitas* comes from "humus," soil—are we able to touch heaven. The person who wants to take heaven by storm, on the other hand, the person of high ideals but without self-knowledge, only encounters his own imaginings, his own projections.

Japanese Zen Master Hisamatsu uses different words, but, to my sense, he describes the same unfathomable process. He puts it more sharply, but it's all about the same paradox of looking for rest *in the heart* of unrest. He starts out from the same recognizable experience. Silence forces us to take stock of our actual manner of being human. And then we hit a wall, a dead point. No matter what we do, no matter what we try, something in us continues to feel lost and estranged, despite the myriad ways of society to meet our human needs. Silence confronts us with an unbearable bottomlessness, and there appears no way out. We have no other choice but to align ourselves with the religious depths in us. But that is exactly where liberation is possible. Just in that impasse, at that dead point, is the miracle accomplished of "resurrection to true life." According to Hisamatsu, there is no way to truly live other than by piercing through the negative. All other ways of living our life are unstable and full of confusion. We have *to work* our way through the negative. That's why in our ordinary way of living, this threat is always with us. And if we don't work through it, we remain prey to fear and dissatisfaction.

About the ineffable experience that occurs within us during this tough sojourn, Hisamatsu says that it resurrects us into true life. Benedict says that it makes us a monk, from the Greek word *monos*—one—and that out of this oneness and peace of heart we return to the world differently. But how? *How* else? What is that true life to which we awaken? It cannot be put into words. Whoever tries will find out. If, nevertheless, I have to put a label on it, I would say: it makes you look at things differently. Things acquire deeper meaning. Because of the silence you start feeling greater responsibility for the manner in which you carry yourself in life. You become more careful in the way you deal with people and things. Through this difficult process you discover that you are connected with everything and everybody. At the same time, you become far less possessive of people and things. You can let them be as they are.

To be at home with ourselves is, thus, extremely difficult, but I experience it as the most meaningful thing we can do. Not to flee from ourselves and that dead point in us. To endure the inner unrest. To wait patiently until the inner turmoil subsides. And to discover with astonishment that in and because of the silence we acquire new eyes, a new heart.

There is one more thing I need to say about this being at home with oneself. Self-knowledge is *the* way to gentleness, understanding, and compassion for those with whom we live and work. As the Desert Fathers say: "He who knows himself, judges nobody."

to practice for others

zazen
sitting
with the quiet
presence
of shadows
unbiased
acceptance
of their existence
motionless
performing
the harmonious dance
of a flock of birds
departing
in the fall
for the same destination

Liliane Priem

When people hear that you practice meditation they often say that "it probably gives you a nice rest," or "it helps you to relax," and so on. I get it. Apparently many people feel that there is something suffocating in our way of living, and therefore they literally search for breathing space. For that matter, I too want to feel good in my skin. Who doesn't? But in reality, for me the path of silence has to do with something else. I often ask myself if meditation for the purpose of feeling better about ourselves (in our life, our work, our relationships) is, in the long run, not equally suffocating? Whether you are imprisoned in your own sorrow or in your own happiness, you are still imprisoned.

In this respect, the sutras have surprised me. It strikes me how Buddhist texts regularly refer to "the other." The Avatamsaka Sutra starts with a sentence that turns sitting in meditation into an authentic relationship with others. "The essence of meditation is the Great Compassion. It is its body, its source, and its means to spread across the whole universe. Without this 'great heart' of love and compassion, meditation, no matter how exalted it may be in other ways, has no meaning at all." The Sutra Dharani of the Great Compassionate One talks about meditation as "responding to the heart that hears the cries of distress," and thus places the act of individual sitting within a perspective of solidarity without boundaries. The Sutra is almost a prayer: "That I may enter into this heart that listens. It is the fullness of all meaning, the ground and purification of all that lives . . ." The one who forgets that meditation is all about engagement, with everything and everybody, is soon enough reminded in the four solemn vows that are recited regularly. The first vow reads: "No matter how numerous the living beings may be, I commit to liberate them all."

The Christian tradition also refers constantly to the other in its description of the path of silence. I am thinking of a well-known saying of Evagrius, a desert monk of the fifth century: "A monk is he who, separated from all, is connected to all." Just like Zen practitioners, Christian monks actively look for silence and sometimes literally go into the desert, precisely the place where we think that everything dries up, to allow love and compassion to flower.

I have spent plenty of time wrestling with that proposition. Many years ago, before I became familiar with abbey life, I saw on the cover of a small book listing the addresses of abbeys the picture of a monk in prayer. The text below read: "This too is a way of love." I did not get it. How could this be? Does love not occur between one person and another? Love requires hands, no? What I saw monks practicing was exactly the opposite: secluding themselves, withdrawing into themselves. For the life of me, I was unable to see what this could have to do with love. "No matter how numerous the living beings may be, I commit to liberate them all"—but isn't it nonsense to utter these words after a simple half hour's meditation, alone by yourself on your mat? What's the point? Because I don't get it.

In the many hours of silence that I have known in my life since then, however, the nonsensical words "separated from all, connected to all" and "I commit to liberate them all," started acquiring meaning. They came, as it were, to life.

What strikes me when I'm in silence, in solitude, during a Zen retreat of several days or at other times, is that there comes a dead point in which everything reverses. Anybody who has really tried to enter deep silence recognizes this scary moment. Meditating can be quite oppressive. It confronts us with a fundamental powerlessness. But precisely in this "standing naked," in stillness, in this couple of square yards of our existence, with all of our limitations, our impotence, our dents and bruises, says the Avatamsaka Sutra, that is where relationship becomes possible. This is the place where compassion is born, across all boundaries, even toward the smallest thing.

The Sutra is like a litany, every sentence beginning with "This is the place . . ." Each time there is an expression of engagement, solidarity, reaching down, if need be even into hell. For example, it says: "This is the place of all those who are marked by love and compassion. When they see the suffering of other living beings, they are ready to go down into this suffering and to experience that exact same pain in themselves."

Is it not there, in hell, where all readymade answers disappear, that true com-passion ("suffering with") becomes possible? A solidarity of the heart, more than of reason and of will. Does a person not become much gentler after having experienced limits and powerlessness? Here we touch upon the mystery of *kenosis*, emptying, and the Sutra suggests that this mystery takes shape at the very place where we are standing or sitting, among all its shards and splinters.

Thus, impotence and loneliness can in silence suddenly be transformed into all-encompassing love. This cannot be forced. It is of a religious nature. No human being can cause it to happen. There is no method to achieve it. It is, to use an old-fashioned word, a grace. It is also not the case that, having one day obtained it, you can put it in your pocket and keep it. Each time you have to make the connection again, you have to search and to wrestle, to stay in the very midst of it, keeping watch and waiting, until—sometimes just for a moment—it opens up. Willingness is important, not experience. The fact of getting started. And then, effortlessly, love will grow hands and feet in our daily life.

According to monastic wisdom, the path of silence is all about engagement, an engagement with everything and everybody. That hit me right from the start, even if I did not understand the first thing about it. Hisamatsu, the great renewer of Japanese Zen, goes a step further than what most people imagine meditation to be. He emphasizes that the first solemn vow is the most profound one and that it has to happen at the start of your journey. It's not about changing yourself first or becoming a better person first before you can do something for somebody else. No, you have to include the other from the very beginning of your practice.

He writes: "We have to practice with a heart that desires to include all other beings in this practice, so that they and you are saved together. We may never simply put ourselves first in our practice, and only then extend our practice to others. We have to go a step further, and reach the point where the practice for ourselves becomes identical with practicing for others. For us human beings, this is something sublime. This kind of love is crucial for religion."

Practicing for others turns our ordinary way of conducting ourselves on its head. To do it, Hisamatsu seems to suggest, it is unnecessary to feel in fine shape or in a harmonious mood. In his eyes, meditation is a religious path, even though Buddhism may not be a religion in the strict sense of the word. I share the concern of certain Zen teachers about the threatening superficiality of Zen in the West. Indian Jesuit and Zen teacher AMA Samy, who visits Belgium each year, says that it worries him to see how meditation is commercialized and consumed here, to which I would add: and individualized—a blind spot in our culture.

Striving after individual happiness stands in contradiction to the basic aspiration of Buddhism, in which it is not about *me* and *mine* but all about *everything and everybody*. The essence of Buddhism is that the "I," in which we normally experience ourselves and with whom we present ourselves to others, does not exist. Our true identity lies elsewhere, in the invisible realm that connects us with everything and everybody. Meditation serves to become aware of this, and this awareness is the basis of a limitless compassion. This is not theory but actual experience. It is revealed to us at the bottom of a lived silence.

Meditation, Zen, and spirituality have to do with a desire for wholeness—and who does not aspire to that? In the silence, this desire is at the same time broken into pieces and broken open. To meditate, to enter the silence, is to venture into the great unknown. If meditation has a beneficial physical, as well as spiritual, effect, then I think of it in this way: as something that blossoms unexpectedly but beyond our grasp in the midst of all the shards and splinters . . . Something new, something unknown, something grand.

bull power

Blessed are they
who know their own weakness.

Isaac the Syrian

I ordered a DVD of animated movie masterpieces on the internet. They are delightful. Little jewels. At times funny, at times absurd, but always artistic and full of worldly wisdom. One particularly impresses me: *The Too Little Prince* [*Le trop petit prince*] by Zoia Trofimova, made in 2001. In some ways it reminds me of the small masterpiece with the nearly identical name by Antoine de Saint-Exupéry. You see a small planet, with one house on it: that of the little prince. But this is where the comparison ends. Trofimova's story is totally different. Her animated movie shows a day in the life of the "too little prince."

It's morning and you see the little prince get up, open the shutters, vacuum the house, etc. Then he briskly steps outside. He looks at the sky and sees—my oh my—stains on the sun. His mood sinks immediately. These ugly stains really bother him. They cannot be left like that. They have to go, and go they shall. You see the little prince busily in action all day long. He tries everything to get to the sun with a broom. He clambers atop a table, climbs to the roof, puts up a ladder, hangs from his toy helicopter, etc. All in vain. The sun triumphantly stays out of reach. But in the evening the sun goes down. It sinks so low that—what joy!—it comes within reach. With great enthusiasm he fetches a pail and a sponge. Well, why did he not think of this earlier? Look, it's going to be so easy. But the stains prove stubborn. As a person possessed the little prince tries to rub the sun clean: from left to right, up and down, then in circles, faster and faster, until finally not the slightest smidgen remains. Shining brilliantly, the sun continues to go down. Her light is so intense that the little prince has to put on a pair of sunglasses. Reflected in the dark lenses you see the sun turning red and slowly sink lower and lower, until she disappears. Contentedly the little prince cleans up his tiny planet and goes inside. He gets ready to go to bed. You hear him flush the toilet and the light is switched off. In the meantime, the movie zooms in on the underside of the little planet. You see a pipe . . . the drainpipe of the toilet, which splatters dirt all over the sun that passes by just then.

There is much to see in this short movie: obsession, fixation, angst, compulsive cleanliness, even the pitiful human tendency to address the wrong problems—all variations of the "too little person." I especially see this in it: there is no life without stains. No matter what we do, our life is and remains partially soiled. The human being is sun and shadow, light and dark. Whether it would be a good thing to try to get rid of the dark appears to me to be an open question.

This reminds me of an article by Andrew Peers, a monk from Zundert, that he wrote for a Zen periodical. In the piece he refers to the "ten pictures of the Ox," which are well-known in the Buddhist world, that represent our human journey. To make a long story short, the path of the ox is really an extended lesson: it's about the searching, finding, seeing, catching, taming, riding, letting go, and forgetting of the ox. The teaching goes even further: back to the source and back to the market. But let's stay with the ox for a moment. The ox is of course only an image for something in us. A sort of dark, ambiguous energy, an inner fire that, as Peers says, can be warming as well as ravaging. And he finds "ox" too weak an image. He prefers to speak of "the bull within us."

Anybody who has ever stood eye to eye with a bull does not exactly think of a sweet tenderness. A bull's energy is fierce and unpredictable. The colossal animal projects such brute force that you wonder how his four short legs can carry it all. Thus, there is a brute force within us that needs to be tamed. But Peers emphasizes that taming is very different from castrating. "Don't cut off his balls," he says in a telling image, "but the images and the objects that the bull is directed to." How so? "By creating space within yourself to receive that energy. By staying with the rawness and the randomness of the energy without trying to kill it, as in a Spanish bullfight, or letting it run amok. By experiencing that energy in its original power before you make a move." It comes down to a consciousness-raising: what do we do to the bull and what does the bull do to us?

People have to fill in for themselves what the bull signifies. I have heard that bull snorting inside of me many times. And even worse than that. Nobody put it better than French theologian Xavier Thévenot when I met him in Paris when still a student: "I thought I was an angel. Then I fell ill and apparently there dwelled a devil within me." And, of course, the illness is not the villain. Crises only reveal that brute force within us in its full power. The bull broke loose within me. A tiny wrong remark, and I went ballistic. Was I ever irrationally incensed! At that time my arms were losing all strength, but that did not stop me from hurling full glasses, bottles, and even chairs against the wall, like a veritable Samson. Snorting and kicking, that bull inside me. I was literally ready to commit murder. So smashing some glass was far and away the least bad thing I could do. Now I can laugh about it but not then. It awakened an enormous despair in me, and deep shame. Was that me?

I am still amazed at how the monk in whom I confided this did not judge me—very much against my expectation. He did not admonish me in the slightest. He appeared not at all shocked. Time and time again he emphasized that there was no other way. As if he wanted to suggest that only with that stain of shame a new light could shine on my life. As far as he was concerned, the ugly stains did not need to be wiped from my sun. Anyway, it would not have worked. It makes no sense to tell a bull "you can't be wild." A bull is a bull. That monk accepted me, exactly as I was. And because of that I could start accepting myself, with stains, bull power, dark side and all, with everything that rose up in me, good or bad. And I have to say: there shone a new light . . .

"Don't judge," says the Sutra of Identity of Multiplicity and Unity. You also find it in the gospels. Does Jesus not say in the parable of the weeds and the grain that it's better to leave the weeds be? These exhortations are not there for nothing. We are accepted, regardless of the judgment of everything and everybody, even if we cannot accept ourselves. For me this realization constituted a turning point. Because I had been unable to accept myself, no way. I had always pursued high ideals, and I felt like a failure. The images I had about being human could not be reconciled with the bull that was carrying on like crazy inside of me. I was ashamed of that inner fury.

But precisely in our failings and all-too-human foibles, a dimension opens up. That monk opened my eyes to it. It's the same ugly bull that can lead us to full life. Because imperfections awaken in us the potential to love. Eye to eye with our brute force and weakness, the impossible demand of the Gospel and the Bodhisattva-vow becomes possible. Only there love is possible for everything and everybody, even for what is broken and failed. How can we tolerate the stains that surround us if we cannot admit our own? "Love your neighbor as yourself," "love your enemies," "pray for those who persecute you," "no matter how numerous the living beings may be, I commit to liberate them all." Impossible commands, each one of them, except *if we see ourselves and accept ourselves as we are.* No soul, and no life, exists without blemishes, and that is a good thing.

In some fashion, we all dream of a "spotless" life. How we imagine this is different for each person. But we are ready to sacrifice a lot for it. In that respect, we're not unlike the "too little prince," perhaps more so than we like. Don't we go through enormous trouble, and don't we busy ourselves to an extraordinary extent, in order to remove the stains from our lives? Is that not what drives us? And, just like the little prince, don't we pursue it with an ingeniousness that borders on the unbelievable? Implicitly we live with this idea: life is good, and if we don't feel good then that's because of the stains. As if something like an unstained life existed, as long as we work hard enough at it. Hammer a little more here, polish a bit more there, smooth out the sharp edges, and we've got it.

But is that really true? Is it not an illusion? More and more I wonder if it is not a serious misconception. Nothing exists under the sun without an opposite: ebb and flow, day and night, light and dark, sun and shadow, peace and war, good and evil, etc. You can continue this list ad infinitum. Perhaps we make a mistake when we take things apart and only associate half of the list with what is real. The negative aspect says perhaps something equally valuable about life's deepest reality. In order to create an electric spark, don't you need two poles, just as it takes both sun *and* rain to create a rainbow? Why then all that effort to cancel out the negative pole?

For me, the story of Elijah exemplifies, time and again, how dynamic life between two poles can be. Elijah, prophet of Israel, friend of God, the epitome of a monk . . . he is tired and depressed. Did he also dream of a pure, unstained life? Was he discouraged that all his efforts came to naught? For forty days and nights he walks to the mountain of Moses in order to withdraw there. He spends the night in a cave of the mountain and all of a sudden there is thunder, lightning, and the earth is shaking. And the text repeats: "And God was not in the thunder, God was not in the lightning, God was not in the earthquake." Then he hears—in Benoît Standaert's translation from the Hebrew—"a voice of a penetrating silence." Could the silence that followed have been so penetrating without all the rumble, blare, and clatter? And in that moment, Elijah covers his face, exits, and goes to meet God.

Elijah retreats in silence. But it doesn't stay quiet very long. Soon all hell breaks loose. The bull throws his weight around. Elijah is confronted with himself and he does not recoil. He learns to accept himself with warmth and gentleness, just as he is. Like a true bodhisattva he creates space to meet the bull. Without moving, he stays put in the rawness and the aimlessness of this brute force, without killing it or driving it away. He sits on the mountain like a mountain, even if there is royal thundering, lightning, and shaking within him. And exactly there, in the not fleeing from all the tumult inside of him *and* in the hearing of the voice of silence, arises the ability to come into relation . . . with God and at the same time with everything and everybody.

The Reality is *one*, even if we need to name it and to experience it in pairs of opposites. The sun is impure. The angel is also a devil. It's unavoidable. But precisely in that tension, there is the spark of life. The unstained life is dead.

not the winter but the duration

We feel and hear the wind
but know nothing about it
not whence it comes
nor where it goes
and if it slows and ceases
we know not where it rests

Willem Iven

In moments of crisis, our head can be so clear. Sometimes we push through to a power that borders on the unbelievable—only to slump into gloom afterward, when the crisis has passed. It's as if suffering intense pain sharpens our attention. It seems that in moments of crisis, all mental energy necessary for battle is bundled into one force aimed solely at the essential. This kind of concentration shakes off secondary concerns like ballast and keeps a single focus on the real thing. When the crisis is over, the clenched attention almost immediately falls apart. All kinds of desires rear up. Before you know it, they all demand their part and once again you are divided and fragmented . . . the plaything of a multitude of little pains and fears. You end up torn in a way that feels worse than the acute pain of the crisis.

To fall ill, to be told you have only one more year to live, to watch your world come crashing down, to lose everything—it was bearable, crazy though that may sound. Sometimes, when we are in crisis we can literally move mountains. It's unbelievable all the things we are capable of. Desert, deprivation, pain, at any time of day or night . . . nothing can subjugate us. Nothing can destroy a person, I thought at the time. Not true. After a terrible struggle with the fragility of this existence, I arrived at a point of pure, simple, naked, abundant, and sheer *being*. Don't ask me how. I can't say a sensible thing about it. But I ended up at a wondrous point of pure being. In the words of John of the Cross: "*Un inmenso ser incubierto en mi alma*" ("An immense being hidden in my soul"). The freedom that opens up in this state of being is as limitless as the power that it unleashes. Having arrived at this remarkable point, I really felt that I could tackle *anything*. The feeling is not permanent, however—for the simple reason that we are unable to reach this godlike point by ourselves. Occasionally, despite ourselves, we are lifted up for a moment to this point of eternity. But soon enough, gravity asserts itself and we slip back down into time. In the case of an incurable illness, that can be a time of "murderous hopelessness." I could only watch passively as the power flowed out of me until, in the miserable circumstances of my life, I was left once again to my own devices.

It's not the winter, not the crisis per se, that breaks a person but the duration—without hope that it will ever end. The long duration pulls you down because a human life is filled with a thousand small desires and, conversely, with a thousand little fears and pains. You cannot live thirty years as if each day is your last. You cannot maintain, year in year out, a single focus on the essence of things, on reality. Certainly not in times like ours in which we are defined by our projects and achievements. In our society, the ungraspable, mysterious essence of things is not what explains and directs our life. It is palpable and tangible desires. Extremely concrete desires that, in my case, can never blossom—they were broken in the bud. Alas, I cannot pull them up by their roots either. How do you live with that? Is it even possible to live with something like that? I don't know. I still hope so. Sometimes I'm afraid it's not.

In the night without end that is my life, I feel challenged by the Benedictine cheerfulness. Monks have a way with it that speaks to my heart. Wil Derkse, Dutch writer and Benedictine oblate, writes: "The dictionary gives the following meanings, among others, to cheerfulness: in good spirits, good-humored, accepting of sorrow and misfortune. This last meaning shows that cheerfulness has to do with courage, namely, the courage to show a positive and infectious élan even in difficult situations." Benedict had insight into human nature. He lived in community and knew darn well how quickly relationships can sour. It seemed to him that there is no greater poison than the eternal tendency of people to complain. Not that there cannot be good reason to complain. But it doesn't help one whit. Benedict thinks concretely. He is concerned with results. Hence his plea to assume a positive attitude in difficult circumstances.

I can't say he's mistaken. Certainly, if there is something seriously wrong in your life, it's easy to find fault with everything and everybody. And it works like poison. "It troubles vision, drains energy, and harms the heart," writes Wil Derkse. "This is true for internal as well as for outward complaining. The person who is grumbling inside no longer sees and hears clearly, because there is another voice that is leading. Complaining outwardly is even more damaging, because it spreads like wildfire. Complainers seek each other's company, they reinforce each other, and they contaminate others."

I am not one to join groups. When dealing with the outside, I'm not too bad. I don't think that most people would consider me a complainer. But inside I have to be extremely firm in shutting down the complaining voice, or my whole life would be infected by it. If I don't muster the courage to show a positive disposition in the difficult circumstances of my life, there would not be much joy left.

The English mystic Evelyn Underhill relates cheerfulness to composure, kindness, and strength, regardless of the exterior circumstances. She writes: "If, then, we desire a simple test of the quality of our spiritual life, a consideration of the tranquility, gentleness and strength with which we deal with the circumstances of our outward life will serve us better than anything that is based on the loftiness of our religious notions, or fervour of our religious feelings. It is a test that can be applied anywhere and at any time. Tranquility, gentleness and strength, carrying us through the changes of weather, the ups and downs of the route, the varied surface of the road; the inequalities of family life, emotional and professional disappointments, the sudden intervention of bad fortune or bad health, the rising and falling of our religious temperature. This is the threefold imprint of the Spirit on the souls surrendered to His great action."

That kind of cheerfulness does not come easy. It does not come of its own accord. You have to work at it. It is as if you have to create a space within which that courage may have a chance. How? By building in silence. By reading something inspiring now and then . . . a poem, a good novel, a mystic. By writing. By developing a sense of humor. By making time for a walk or for music. For other people perhaps it is working in the garden, painting, sculpting, or something else altogether. In other words, it has to do with working at expanding your horizons, with looking for situations in which stillness and contemplation can flourish—not just occasionally but regularly.

For me, silence is the most important thing of all, even if I have to confess that I often avoid it. I don't always dare to engage in the naked confrontation with an equally bare despondency. Sometimes I avoid the silence out of pure anger. Because I cannot get over the fact that I was denied a normal life among people my age. Even so, there is also the urge to build in moments of silence . . . in order not to drown in the endless dark waters of pain and sorrow, in order to maintain a connection with the infinite being that is hidden deep inside of us. Thomas Merton puts it well: "There is more consolation in the heart of stillness than in an answer to a question." But you don't have that consolation in your pocket. You can't force it. Sometimes you have it; oftentimes you have to do without.

I wish I had sufficient strength to write with regularity. Writing is a powerful weapon in the struggle. It doesn't enable you to vanquish despair, but it certainly helps to stay standing. And in the process of writing you sometimes bump into a wondrous hope. As the Jewish-Hungarian writer Imre Kertész wrote in the midst of dark and heavy pages: "I write in the hope someday to get to know my hope." Kertész was deported to Auschwitz as a fourteen-year-old boy and survived the holocaust.

Reading helps, more than anything else. It takes courage to search out silence or to write, and courage often fails me. And then not much happens. But a book is usually doable, and it always works. Literature that feeds you. Words that ensure that you do not close up, that you do not choke in despair. Words that speak truth to life, *as it is*. Words as food and drink—after all, you have to get the strength to go on from somewhere! Passionate words. In any event, no answers. Answers can only diminish the mystery, while true words enlarge it. Answers reduce words to ends in themselves, final destinations. The strength of answers lies only in serving our self-righteousness or the needs of our (laboriously constructed) ego. While words can simply be stepping stones to risk the jump, right into the living mystery . . . not to anywhere in particular, always farther. True words confront us with our not-knowing, with our inability, and in the paltriness of this not-knowing and this inability, they open us up to an infinite horizon.

I can feel enormously fortified by what I read in other people's writings. I don't think that I could endure the night of my life without the daily company of words. The art of the deal is to develop the discipline of letting yourself be accompanied day after day by the words of others. Patiently learning to live by the word, like the monks. Living by the age-old wisdom distilled out of the rawness and the beauty of life.

In this connection, here is a passage in the work of German theologian Karl Rahner that I find challenging: "Have we tried to love God in those places where one is not carried on a wave of emotional rapture, where it's impossible to mistake oneself and one's life-force for God, where one accepts to die from a love that seems like death and absolute negation, where one cries out in an apparent emptiness and an utter unknown?" These words provoke me enormously as, in my intuitive understanding, they seem to say that a path is only worthwhile if you continue on it, even if from time to time it meanders through a no-man's-land. What is the value of my path with and in silence if I follow it just because it consoles? In that case, am I not seeking myself in lieu of the silence? Don't I then get caught again in "wanting to pull everything to myself?" Does the wind become less enchanting because it has calmed down and can no longer be felt? Or does it not become even more enchanting in this completely ungraspable coming and going?

Han Fortmann also challenges me. He writes: "It's all about discovering how often you have to say 'yes' to so much brokenness. 'Yes,' also, to the realization that the broken pieces remain. That you have to pick them up every day, and carry them along for another day, day in day out. Broken pieces—only heaven sees the depth of their radiance. This is wholeness in the sense of religious salvation and I can only translate it by faith, hope, and love." Without being able to explain why and without a sense of immediate comfort, I feel that these words are true. They engage me on a deeper level. Now, on a shallower level I wish not to have anything to do with these words and I only want to be angry and unhappy about every mishap. That struggle is my life. That choice. Not between working through the pain (and then be done with it) or staying with the pain. The pain is there anyway and it is constant. The choice is between two levels of dealing with it: hardened revolt, unlivable bitterness, eternal complaining; or to accept the pain again and again, day after day, falling and getting up, in faith, hope, and love.

Another thing that helps is walking. Preferably in nature. Preferably alone. Or with somebody but in silence. Nothing is as glorious as being blown about by the wind, literally and figuratively. If done in silence, you establish contact with nature: the rustle of the wind through the leaves, the smell of oak in the forest, the blackbird busy with twigs . . . it puts things in perspective. It changes oppression into breathing space. Every single time.

Music helps. Especially if it's born out of silence, like Russian Orthodox or classical music. There is a contemporary composer whose music really moves me: John Tavener. A while ago I saw him interviewed on television. He talked about the fact that the ego was introduced into music with the Renaissance and that we are now, with the cult of pop stars, experiencing the limits of that. Before, ego did not exist. All music was religious. Tavener deplores that evolution. Composing is, for him, a religious matter and you hear it in his music. I can listen to it for hours.

Humor helps more than anything. I remember a party at which somebody who did not know me asked whether I was left- or right-handed. Both of my arms are paralyzed and I did not know what to say. A friend quickly came to my rescue: "Oh, she's simply not handy at all." Kahlil Gibran says somewhere: "I want no part of a wisdom that knows no tears, a philosophy that cannot laugh, and a greatness that does not bend down to children." That's also why I am so enthralled by the Zen talks of Ton Lathouwers. They are splashed with humor. Wisdom that lacks in humor cannot be trusted, I think. But if well-seasoned with humor, I appreciate it, no matter its provenance. There is a funny story about the vexing question of evil in the world. I believe I heard it during a storytelling performance of Hasidic tales by Dutch preacher Nico ter Linden.

One fine day, the people decide there's really too much evil in creation and they decide to bring God to justice. They draw up two columns: one for all the wrongs committed by human beings and the other for all the wrongs attributed to the Almighty. Then they start discussing and taking notes. The columns fill up, now on the left side, then on the right. After a while the people conclude they have pretty well covered it. All the big problems that cause mankind to struggle have been talked about and have been allocated to one column or another. They take a step back, look at the total picture, and say to each other and to the Almighty: "Oh well, it's just about even-steven, forget about it."

This little story does not resolve anything and it does not provide any answers, but through its playfulness, humor, and simplicity, it makes you smile and opens up something inside.

short story about love

All authentic life
is encounter.

Martin Buber

In his book *Everything Is Love* [*Alles is liefde*] Pieter van der Meer writes: "I cannot rid myself of the thought that every encounter with a human being has meaning, that it causes ascertainable even though usually undetectable consequences, and hence that it must have meaning in the plan of God's creation—whether the encounter is as fleeting as catching someone's eye, the first time strangers speak each other's name, or becomes a lifelong union until the last goodbye in preparation for the eternal encounter."

His words contrast with the key passage in the novel *Night Train to Lisbon* by Pascal Mercier. In this fragment, the precariousness of the human condition is expressed by the metaphor of a train. Amadeu, the main character, writes in his diary:

> One day in the distant past I woke up in my compartment and felt rolling. It was exciting. I listened to the pounding of the wheels, held my head in the wind and savored the speed of things passing by me. . . . It was in Coimbra, on a hard bench in the lecture hall that I became aware: I can't get off. I can't change the tracks or the direction. I don't determine the pace. I don't see the locomotive and can't see who's driving it and whether the engineer makes a reliable impression. . . .

> I can't change the compartment. In the corridor, I see people passing by and think: Maybe it looks completely different in their compartment than in mine. But I can't go there and see, a conductor I never saw and never will has bolted and sealed the compartment door. I open the window, lean far out and see that everybody else is doing the same thing. The train makes a soft curve. The last cars are still in the tunnel and the first are going on. Maybe the train is traveling in a circle, over and over, without anybody noticing it. I see all the others craning their neck to see and understand something. I call a greeting, but the wind blows away my words.

Who of these two is right? Certainly, Paul Mercier is not wrong with his cynical image of the train. He expresses something recognizable, in today's society perhaps more than ever. The fact of being defined, of being put on a track, before we could choose for ourselves. Our not-knowing and not-understanding of life. The experience that it's not so simple to make contact with people. Misunderstandings crop up quickly, and more often we talk past one another rather than to each other. And I am not even talking about psychological mechanisms such as projection, repression, and displacement that poison intercourse among people and render it impossible. Indeed, the depressing question is raised whether encounter is possible at all.

Yet, the words of Mercier do not cover the whole range of what it means to be a human person. Not that I would go as far as Pieter van der Meer. For me it is not so clear how it all works with "God" and an alleged plan of creation. Now, I would like to be able to affirm that vision. But that *every* encounter is fraught with meaning—that I can't say. Nevertheless, it does more for me than the image of a train aimlessly racing along in circles, in which encounter is excluded by definition. Besides the absurd in life, there is the experience of something else. For me, there is an "and yet." I would prefer to give a more circumspect answer, one that is more nuanced, using Martin Buber's beautiful phrase: "All authentic life is encounter."

Not everything is love. There are things that are just impossible to reconcile with encounter and love. I am thinking of the German movie *Beautiful Bitch* about Romanian street kids who become ensnared in a human trafficking network. They are locked up, abused, and forced to commit street crime. That is just one example. What does these kids' painful reality have to do with "everything is love" and "I cannot rid myself of the thought that every encounter with a human being has meaning?"

Buber is more realistic. Not all life is encounter. Only *authentic* life is encounter. His words do justice to both dimensions of life: the potentiality *and* the difficulty. Encounter does not happen just like that. It presupposes alertness, openness to the *authentic*, and requires really working on ourselves. And it is true: in each authentic encounter, there is a spark of the ultimate Reality. But if I look back on my life, I have to admit that I have also suffered from contact with people. I still do today, even if it is not as extreme as for those Romanian street urchins. Yet, there is also the experience that true encounter is possible, and that the power of such encounters *endures*—cognizably and untraceably.

During moments when it's a question of life or death it is of critical importance to have people around you and to know that they will pick you up. You see it in *Beautiful Bitch*. It's the only thing that makes the movie somewhat bearable. The Romanian Bica—nicknamed "Bitch"—is "picked up" by a few German youths. It gives the young girl the strength to take matters into her own hands, regardless of how difficult it proves to be to stay out of the clutches of the gang leader. The German Milka and her friends are moved by Bica. They are touched by "the face of the other." Maybe this expression of Levinas comes closest to what makes a life an "authentic" life and encounter: regard for the other. Who picks up whom does not matter. Sometimes you are the one who does the picking up. Sometimes you are the one who needs to be picked up. And it is an open question whether there is something like being picked up while picking up, and vice versa. Real encounter is always reciprocal. That is also something you see in the movie. At a certain moment, it is no longer clear who picks up whom: Milka Bica or Bica Milka.

I experienced the saving aspect of the presence of another stronger than ever during the period in which my life became like drifting sand and I hit rock bottom. I am thinking of two encounters. There were others, but these two stand out. Without these encounters, I would not have survived. Without them I would never have found the strength to take my mutilated life in my own hands. The first one took place while I was in the student movement. I was the leader at the time my illness began, and I confided in somebody. He was the first person to whom I disclosed the terror of what was going on in my body. That person became my best friend. I married him. I will never forget how he traveled the difficult path at my side throughout that dark period. He never filled in for me. He simply was *present*. He let me rage and kick, time and again. At the same time he encouraged me to endure the emptiness. He refused to look for a way out for me. He repeated constantly that the only person who could find an answer was me. His attitude moved me profoundly. "How? what? where? when? I don't know," he wrote. "The journey through no-man's-land is long, the end not in sight. But hang in there, Bieke, hang in there." For months and months these words were the only thing that kept me going, right through the night.

The second encounter was shorter but made an equally lasting impression. In that same period, one evening I took the last train in Leuven for Kortrijk. There was an announcement that the trains were running slow due to a strike, but being in a daze under the blow of my illness, I missed it. As a result, I arrived way too late at the station of Ghent, where I had to catch my connection. There were no more trains. For me that was the proverbial straw that broke the camel's back. I crashed. In a total mess, I collapsed on a bench and could not stop crying. Even today I am moved thinking how a total stranger sat down next to me. He did not say a word. He simply kept sitting next to me in silence, an hour long, while I wept. When I stopped crying, he asked: "Is there anything I can do for you?" I gave him my parents' telephone number. He found a telephone booth and called them, asking that they come pick me up, and remained with me until they arrived. Just like that, in the middle of the night, in the Ghent railway station. We did not exchange a word. But it was one of the most impressive encounters of my life.

Encounters like that are a gateway. They open onto *every* other, no matter where, no matter whom. The fact of the matter is that real encounters work U-turns. By having been picked up, you become somebody who can pick up others. They are "short stories about love," and perhaps they are rare. But they exist, without a doubt. And when the epic tales no longer serve, they always do.

glossary

Bodhisattva: In the Mahayana tradition: somebody who devotes his or her life to the welfare and liberation of all living beings.

Buddha: "Shakyamuni" means: the wise one in the Shakya lineage. Proper name: Siddharta Gautama. Siddharta Gautama lived in the sixth century BC in India. He is often called "the Buddha" or "Buddha" for short. Buddha means "the awakened (enlightened) one."

Ch'an: Chinese translation of the Sanskrit word "dhyana," which means Zen or meditation. In the sixth century BC, Shakyamuni had the experience of inner awakening. His teachings spread throughout all of India, primarily as a result of the work of the Indian monk Bodhidharma, around AD 500. The teachings became known in China under the name ch'an. The **Maha Karuna Ch'an**, under the leadership of Zen teacher Ton Lathouwers, unites meditation groups in Flanders and the Netherlands in a loose cooperative framework and is based on the Chinese Ch'an.

Dharma: Buddhist teachings.

Kinhin: Walking meditation, often in-between two sitting meditations.

Koan: In the ch'an and Zen tradition: a word, sentence, or short story, meant as a "life question," challenging someone to a totally unique and personal answer.

Kwan Yin: Chinese: "She who listens to the cries of distress": Bodhisattva of Infinite Compassion. Her important role in Chinese Buddhism strongly resembles that of the Holy Mother in the West.

Maha karuna: The Great Compassion.

Mahayana: Buddhism has two branches: Theravada and Mahayana. In Theravada (which in Pali means the "teachings of the elders") more emphasis is put on individual liberation. In Mahayana (literally "the big vehicle") priority is given to, and the effort necessary for, the liberation of all reality. Zen is a branch of Mahayana Buddhism.

Nirvana: This Sanskrit word renders an important concept in Buddhism. It indicates the highest state of consciousness that a person can achieve.

Novitiate: The formation process to become a monk (in Christian contemplative abbeys and convents).

Oblate: Oblates are laypeople who wish to be inspired by the spirit of the Rule of Benedict and who, by taking a vow, associate themselves with a specific Benedictine abbey.

Psalm: The psalms are a collection of 150 poetic texts. The word "psalm" is of Greek origin and refers to "a song to be sung to the accompaniment of a string instrument." In the Hebrew Bible, the book is called *Tehillim*, Songs of Praise. That title indicates that the entire book of Psalms, including its songs of lamentation, is a polyphonic song of praise to the God of Israel. The book was much read in ancient Judaism and the early days of Christianity. It occupies a central role in abbey choral prayer to this day.

Sangha: Generally, a community of Buddhists; in particular, a community of Zen practitioners.

Sesshin: A Zen retreat spanning several days.

Sutra: Traditional Buddhist text. Text attributed to the Buddha. Certain sutras are recited at meditation meetings.

Teisho: Address by a Zen teacher during a sesshin.

Zazen: The practice of sitting meditation; sitting in silence and mindfulness.

Zen: Japanese corruption of the Chinese word "ch'an," which in turn is a corruption of the Sanskrit word "dhyana," meaning "meditation."

bibliography

Over the course of the years, I have collected a good many thoughts and quotations that are meaningful to me. Since I did not intend to publish them, I did not always write down the source. Consequently, this bibliography is not complete. I researched as much as I could but was unable to find the source of certain quotations. Since they are (and were) important, I decided nevertheless to include them in the book.

books

Albom, Mitch. *Tuesdays with Morrie*. New York: Broadway Books, 2002.

Andreus, Hans. *Verzamelde gedichten*. Amsterdam: Bert Bakker, 1993.

Anonymous. *The Cloud of Unknowing*. New York: Paulist Press, 1981.

Armstrong, Karen. *Buddha*. New York: Viking Penguin, 2001.

Balmary, Marie. *Abel. Dwars door Eden*. Averbode, Belgium: Altiora, 2000/Kampen, The Netherlands: Kok, 2000.

Barry, Sebastian. *A Long Long Way* (p. 4). New York: Penguin Books, 2006.

Bentounès, Sheikh Khaled. *Sufism: The Heart of Islam*. Translated by Khaled El Abdi. Arizona: Hohm Press, 2002.

Braekers, Marcel. *Meister Eckhart. Mysticus van het niet-wetende weten*. Averbode, Belgium: Altiora, 2007.

Čapek, Karel. *An Ordinary Life*. Translated by M. and R. Weatherall. North Haven, CT: Catbird Press, 1990.

Coninck, Herman de. *De gedichten*. Amsterdam, Antwerpen: De Arbeiderspers, 1998.

Daniel-Ange, ed. *Vuren in the woestijn* (selected texts). Andenne, Belgium: N. V. Magermans, 1988.

Dejager, Jenny. *De smaak van stilte. Gedichten*. Kuurne: uitgave in eigen beheer. Self-published, 1988.

Derkse, Wil. *Een levensregel voor beginners. Benedictijnse spiritualiteit voor het dagelijks leven*. Tielt, Belgium: Lannoo, 2000.

———. *Gezegend leven. Benedictijnse richtlijnen voor wie naar goede dagen verlangt*. Tielt, Belgium: Lannoo, 2007.

Dinnissen, Elizabeth. *Wegen naar helende aandacht. Zazen en beschouwing*. Heeswijk, The Netherllands: Dabar-Luyten, 2002.

Dolto, Françoise. *Vrijgemaakt om te beminnen*. IJsselstein-Antwerpen: Unistad, 1983.

Domek, Johanna. *Benedictijnse inspiratie*. Kampen, The Netherlands: Ten Have, 2006/Averbode, Belgium: Altiora, 2006.

Dostoevsky, Fyodor. *The Brothers Karamazov*. Translated by Richard Pevear and Larissa Volokhonsky. New York: Farrar, Strauss & Giroux, 1990.

Germain, Sylvie. *Les échos du silence*. Paris: Desclée de Brouwer, 1996.

Grün, Anselm. *De hemel begint in jezelf. De wijsheid van de woestijnvaders voor mensen van vandaag*. Kampen, The Netherlands: Ten Have, 2006/Averbode, Belgium: Altiora, 2006.

Grün, Anselm, and Meinrad Dufner. *Spiritualiteit van anderen*. Kampen, The Netherlands: Kok, 1997/Gent, Belgium: Carmelitana, 1997.

Grün, Anselm, and Friedrich Assländer. *Spiritueel leidinggeven*, Tielt, Belgium: Lannoo, in co-editie met [in copublication with] Kampen, The Netherlands: Ten Have, 2007.

Harpman, Jacqueline. *Het strand van Oostende*. Berchem (Antwerpen): EPO, 1998.

Kertész, Imre. *Kaddish for a Child Not Born* (p. 33). Translated by Christopher C. Wilson and Katharina M. Wilson. Evanston, IL: Northwestern University Press, 1997.

Kuijken, Sigiswald, and Marleen Thiers. *Op de Jacobsberg. Pelgrimeren op oneindig*. Tielt, Belgium: Lannoo, 2007.

Lasalle, Enomiya. *Meditatie en godservaring*. Nijmegen, The Netherlands: Gottmer, 1984.

Lathouwers, Ton. *Kloppen waar geen poort is*. Rotterdam: Asoka, 2007.

———. *More Than Anyone Can Do: Zen Talks*. Translated by Mical Goldfarb Sikkema. Amsterdam: VU University Press, 2013.

Levering, Miriam. *Zen Inspirations: Essential Meditations and Texts*. New York: Chartwell Books, 2013.

Libbrecht, Ulricht. *Is God dood?* Tielt: Lannoo, 2004.

Louf, André. *Tuning In to Grace: The Quest for God*. Translated by John Vriend. Kalamazoo, MI: Cistercians Publications, 1992.

Mercier, Pascal. *Night Train to Lisbon* (pp. 369–70 and 424–25). Translated by Barbara Harshav. New York: Grove Press, 2008.

Okri, Ben. *Astonishing the Gods* (pp. 14–15). London: Phoenix, 1996.

Oosterhuis, Huub. *De onrust van de liefde. Gedichten 1983–1993*. Baarn, The Netherlands: De Prom, 1994.

Pessoa, Fernando (Albert Caeiro). *De hoeder van kudden*. Translated by A. Willemsen. Amsterdam: Arbeiderspers, 2003.

———. *The Book of Disquiet*. Translated by Richard Zenith. New York: Penguin Classics, 2002.

Renodeyn, Stef. *De mens die ik ben*. Roeselare, Belgium: Roularta Books, 2007.

Rilke, Rainer Maria. *Letters to a Young Poet*. Translated by M. D. Herter Norton. New York: W. W. Norton & Company, 1993.

Samy, AMA. *Waarom kwam Boddhidharma naar het Westen? De ontmoeting van zen met het Westen*. Nieuwerkerk a/d Ijssel: Asoka, 1998.

———. *Zen: Awakening to Your Original Face*. CreateSpace Independent Publishing Platform, 2012.

Scholtens, Wim R. *"Kijk, hier barst de taal . . .", mystiek bij Kierkegaard*. Kampen, The Netherlands: Kok, 1991/Averbode, Belgium: Altiora, 1991.

Sjöstrand, Östen. *Aan de uiterste grens: gedichten*. Leuven: Leuvense schrijversaktie, 1990.

Smelik, Klaas A. D., ed. *Etty: The Letters and Diaries of Etty Hillesum, 1941–1943*. Translated by Arnold J. Pomerans. Grand Rapids, MI: Eerdmans Publishing Company, 2002.

Smit, Gabriël. *Gedichten*. Bilthoven: Ambo, 1975.

Sölle, Dorothee. *Mystiek en verzet. Gij stil geschreeuw*. Baarn, The Netherlands: Ten Have, 1998.

Standaert, Benoît. *In de school van de psalmen*. Gent, Belgium: Carmelitana, 2009.

———. *Spiritualiteit als levenskunst. Alfabet van een monnik.* Tielt, Belgium: Lannoo, 2010.

Suzuki, Shunryu. *Zen-begin. Eindeloos met zen beginnen.* Deventer, The Netherlands: Ankh-Hermes, 1976.

Tellegen, Toon. *Er ligt een appel op een schaal.* Amsterdam: Querido, 2002.

———. *Miniscule oorlogen (niet met het blote oog zichtbaar).* Amsterdam: Querido, 2004.

———. *Mischien wisten zij alles.* Amsterdam, Antwerpen: Querido, 1996.

Törnqivst, Marit. *Klein verhaal over liefde.* Amsterdam, Antwerpen: Querido, 2000.

Underhill, Evelyn. *Practical Mysticism: A Little Book for Normal People.* New York: Cosimo Classics, 2006.

———. *The Spiritual Life* (pp. 76–77). Harrisburg, PA: Morehouse Publishing, 1937.

Unno, Taitetso. *River of Fire, River of Water: An Introduction to the Pure Land Tradition of Shin Buddhism.* New York: Doubleday, 1998.

Van Broeckhoven, Egied. *Dagboek van de vriendschap.* Brugge: Emmaüs, 1971.

Van het Kruis, Johannes. *Mystieke werken.* Gent, Belgium: Carmelitana, 1992. [For English readers, see Kieran Kavanaugh, ed. *John of the Cross: Selected Writings.* New York: Paulist Press, 1988; and *The Collected Works of St. John of the Cross.* Rev. ed. Translated by Kieran Kavanaugh and Otilio Rodriguez. Washington, DC: ICS Publications, 1991.]

Van Schagen, J. C. *Ik ga maar en ben.* Amsterdam: G. A. van Oorschot, 1971.

Verzameld liedboek. Liturgische gezangen op teksten van Huub Oosterhuis. Kampen, The Netherlands: Kok, 2004/Antwerpen: Halewijn, 2004.

Waaijman, Kees. *De mystieke aanraking.* Kampen, The Netherlands: Ten Have, 2008.

———. *Mystiek in de psalmen.* Kampen, The Netherlands: Ten Have, 2004/Gent, Belgium: Carmelitana, 2004.

Weil, Simone. *Waiting for God* (p. 40). Translated by Emma Craufurd. New York: Harper Perennial Modern Classics, 2009.

Yourcenar, Marguerite. *With Open Eyes: Conversations with Matthieu Galey.* Translated by Arthur Goldhammer. Boston: Beacon Press, 1984.

articles

Chialà, Sabino. "Nederigheid en medelijden, krachtlijnen van Isaaks denken." *Heiliging* 47, no. 4 (1997).

Houwen, Tim. "Interview/Je verveelt je als 't goed gaat." *Trouw* (February 15, 2007).

Olivera, Bernardo. "De lusteloosheid die ons verlangen naar God aantast." *Contactblad Mertonvrienden* 22, no. 2 (June 2008).

Peers, Andrew. "Rodeo Mozes: De zachtmoedigheid en het vuur van de eerste Boddhisattva Gelofte." *Maha Karuna Bericht*, no. 3 (2008).

Renodeyn, Stef. "Het nulpunt: vertrouwen en actie." *Maha Karuna Bericht*, no. 3 (2007).

Stahlie, Maria. "Vol van vervoering en vol van wanhoop." *NRC Handelsblad* 6 (January 2007).

Vandekerckhove, Bieke. "Omtuimelen in God. Zondaars gevraagd." *Tertio* 13 (August 2008).

———. "Schatkist in schatkist in schatkist. In de leer bij Syrische monniken." *Tertio* 28 (May 2008).

websites

www.alsliga.be

www.sintsixtus.be

www.liobaklooster.nl

www.sint-andriesabdij.org

www.abdijmariatoevlucht.nl

www.monasterechevetogne.com

www.mahakarunachan.be

http://zensangha.be

translator's note

This translation follows the author's capitalization practices. It may give the work an unfamiliar appearance, just as it would have appeared uncommon to the reader in the original Dutch language. This is a largely a matter of form rather than substance, although it may provide a signal that the book is about something unfamiliar, something that goes against the grain. In any event, the author's choice of form, particularly, of course, if it carries an implied message, deserves to be respected.

The book contains several quotations from the Bible. Instead of making my own translations of these quotes, I have endeavored to use the text of Bible editions approved by Roman Catholic authorities for use in the United States. Consistency is normally a virtue in translation, and this would indicate the need to use the same Bible edition throughout. At times, however, I found that the author's point or illustration by use of a biblical reference was weaker in one English translation and stronger in another. I opted for the translation that, in my judgment, most fully corresponded to the Dutch biblical text and the author's intent. So, the references are:

Page 11, Psalm 27: *The New Revised Standard Version* Bible. © 1989, Division of Christian Education of the National Council of the Churches of Christ in the United States of America.

Page 12, Psalm 81: *Saint Joseph New Catholic Edition*, Catholic Book Publishing Company (1962); Psalm 137: *The New Jerusalem Bible* (Reader's ed.), Doubleday, 1990.

Page 42, Hosea 2:16: *The New Jerusalem Bible* (Reader's ed.), Doubleday, 1990.

Page 121, Wisdom of Solomon 7:24: *The New Revised Standard Version* Bible. © 1989, Division of Christian Education of the National Council of the Churches of Christ in the United States of America.

With respect to the NRSV, I used the *Saint John's Bible*, published by the Order of Saint Benedict, Collegeville, MN. Its magnificent calligraphy and illuminations lift the spirit and deepen the reader's experience with the text.

There are a number of references to, and quotations from, books the author read in Dutch (or, occasionally, French). If a published English translation of such books exists, accessible through readily available publication channels, I have used only the title of the work in English, and the full reference to the translated work is provided in the bibliography. If no published translation could readily be found, I have given the English translation of the work's title with, in square brackets, the title in the language read by the author, which corresponds to the detailed reference in the bibliography.

This translation was a work of love. I first undertook it because I believe *the taste of silence* will be of material help to Christina, one of my daughters, who suffers from multiple sclerosis, a debilitating chronic disease. As I deepened my familiarity with the book, I became convinced that its spiritual messages could be of significant benefit to anybody, whether the reader is afflicted with illness or is in the best of health. This conviction provided an additional incentive, if any was needed, to complete the translation in a manner suitable for publication.

Rudolf V. Van Puymbroeck

December 28, 2014